Lifestyle Worship

Lifestyle Worship

The Worship God Intended Then and Now

DAVID V. ADAMS

RESOURCE *Publications* · Eugene, Oregon

LIFESTYLE WORSHIP
The Way God Intended Then and Now

Copyright © 2010 David V. Adams. All rights reserved. Except for brief quotations in critical publications or reviews, no part of this book may be reproduced in any manner without prior written permission from the publisher. Write: Permissions, Wipf and Stock Publishers, 199 W. 8th Ave., Suite 3, Eugene, OR 97401.

All scripture quotations, unless otherwise indicated, are taken from the Holy Bible, New International Version®, NIV®. Copyright ©1973, 1978, 1984 by Biblica, Inc.™ Used by permission of Zondervan. All rights reserved worldwide.

Scripture quotations taken from the New American Standard Bible®, Copyright © 1960, 1962, 1963, 1968, 1971, 1972, 1973, 1975, 1977, 1995 by The Lockman Foundation used by permission.

Scripture quotations marked "NKJV™" are taken from the New King James Version®. Copyright © 1982 by Thomas Nelson, Inc. Used by permission. All rights reserved.

Scripture taken from the New Century Version. Copyright © 2005 by Thomas Nelson, Inc. Used by permission. All rights reserved.

Scripture quotations from THE MESSAGE. Copyright © by Eugene H. Peterson 1993, 1994, 1995, 1996, 2000, 2001, 2002. Used by permission of NavPress Publishing Group.

Resource Publications
An Imprint of Wipf and Stock Publishers
199 W. 8th Ave., Suite 3
Eugene, OR 97401
www.wipfandstock.com

ISBN 13: 978-1-60899-583-7

Manufactured in the U.S.A.

To my wonderful wife Theresa,
whose love and sacrifice are the
shining examples of Lifestyle Worship in action.

Contents

Foreword by Margaret Becker • ix
Acknowledgments • xi
Introduction • xiii

PART ONE   CONTEMPORARY WORSHIP
1. Worship Here, Worship There • 3
2. Palmolive Prayers • 25
3. The Act of Worship • 43

PART TWO   LIFESTYLE WORSHIP
4. The A.D.D. Saint • 69
5. Know God • 89
6. Disturbances • 110

Appendix • 123
Glossary • 131
Bibliography • 135

Foreword

WHEN I first read the title of Dave's work, I have to admit—I was not prepared. "Worship" is big business these days in the church. There are so many materials in the market place with the word "worship" somewhere in the description it's overwhelming. And devaluing. Devaluing because the word has become a secret wink, a metaphor for sincerity and the appearance of God's "nod" and participation. It's almost as if somewhere a Pastor, a marketing team, a writer is furrowing their brows in earnest with each title—each description—*worship meeting, worship concert, worship with us* meaning, *we really mean it. God is in this.*

"Worship" has become the code word for validity and sincerity. It's like getting your Doctorate on-line from Barbados for fifty-dollars. It's a shortcut to legitimacy, the title without the arduous journey; the everyday practice of study and assimilation it takes to master a field.

Another book on worship. Another five-steps to this blessing, or ten steps to overcome that obstacle. It's what I think of immediately when someone recommends a title with "worship" in it. It's a little bit what I expected from Dave the first time he contacted me about this work.

It's not what I received.

Envision a man who stopped life midway through and decided to devote years to understanding and communicating the full spectrum of "worship." Understand the lengths that person would have to go to in order to secure the real title of "Doctorate" in that field.

Years of reaching have brought Dave a unique perspective on worship. It is a perspective that in my opinion restores some of the dignity to the overused term itself.

These well-researched thoughts will challenge everyone who exposes themselves to them. These counter-cultural thoughts will deepen and enhance anyone's understanding of worship. Truly, if we as a post-modern church could return to some of these core tenets in whole life worship, I truly believe we would revolutionize our present history, and leave a firm imprint of Christ lived out in our communities.

As you enjoy this book, hopefully you will be a little more prepared than I was for the rich content found here. But let's go one step further, shall we? Let's make an agreement to apply these time-tested truths to our own lives, to walk out Jesus everyday—worshipfully, with mind soul and heart. Let's start that journey here, together with Dave in Lifestyle Worship.

—Margaret Becker

Acknowledgments

In addition to my parent's, Lynn and Lavonne Adams, who have been my role models for living out, before my eyes, an unwavering lifestyle dedicated to worshipping God, I would like to thank the following people that have helped contribute to this book:

My personal Editor, Emily Clare; Julie Roberts Photography (back cover photo); to Jeff F., Melanie M., Madelyn K., and Sherry F. for your tireless and selfless acts; to John Zuck and Glen Davis; and of course M.B., for without you this book would not be possible.

Introduction

WITH THE onslaught of recently published books addressing worship issues, the popular concept of worship can be misleading. The Hebrews of the Old Testament and the believers of the New Testament had a much different understanding of worship. Worship is a lifestyle and not limited to geography or time.

If we offer God our time and resources, we can change our life and the lives of those we come in contact with. In his wonderful book, Prayer: finding the heart's true home, Richard Foster says that,

> ". . . we will never *have* time for prayer—we must *make* time."

Sometimes we must fight for that time, but we must keep moving forward. We must continue to deepen our intimacy with God.

Worship is a way of life. To experience God means that we may have to change our lifestyle. We may have to make hard choices that require the expenditure of energy. It is easy to plop in front of your TV after a harried day, or sit at your computer and get lost in cyberspace. It takes energy to turn the TV off, shut the computer down, and get on our knees. We can never truly experience God until we have spent quality time with him.

If I could sum up the tone of this book, I would say, "God is passionate for us to have passion for him." I don't mean this to sound like a cute cliché for God truly wants us to have a deep, intimate relationship with him. Do you have a passion for him? He's waiting for you.

Part One

Contemporary Worship

1

Worship Here, Worship There

The lights dim as the pianist plays a slow, worshipful melody. A young man standing on the right side of the platform begins to strum his acoustic guitar. A drummer carefully brushes his high hat, while the bass player quietly plunks a B-flat. The lead vocalist steps up to the microphone and begins to softly sing, leading the congregation in a reverent chorus of praise to God. Many worshippers raise their hands heavenward; eyes closed, bodies swaying, lips mouthing unintelligible words. Kari is one of the participants who raises their arms, eyes closed, quietly singing in one accord.

The music slowly fades to a whispered decrescendo. Not allowing an uncomfortable silence, a young man steps to the podium and gives a quick, "Praise God", and proceeds to give the morning announcements, followed by the offering. After the money has been collected, the Minister steps forward and delivers his five-point sermon. After the sermon, a quick chorus announces that this worship experience is completed.

Kari leaves the building feeling rejuvenated. She remembers very little of the sermon, but the experience of singing with a congregation of like-minded people gives her a warm feeling inside. One of the worship choruses rolls around in her head. She tries hard to remember the words and sing it under her breath as she walks her daughters to her car.

Monday morning arrives and Kari quickly scurries to get her daughters off to school and ready herself for work. She overslept and forgot to do her 15-minute devotional. "Oh well, I'll do it tomorrow," she rationalizes. Throughout the week her mind wanders to the wonderful time of worship and she longs for Sunday to come so she can re-live her experience.

This fictional account of Kari's worship experience is sadly all too real. The concept of modern Christian worship found in European and North American churches is delineated by geography, time, and purpose. Specific buildings or places are identified as appropriate venues to participate in a worship experience. A specific day and time are set aside to meet with like-minded congregants. This experience is commonly limited to music and/or liturgy and is usually monitored by an interval of time. Once the musical or liturgical experience has ended, the participant may leave the venue with a satisfied feeling that his/her purpose for worshipping has been fulfilled and defined by a pivotal point in time. But is this how God intended for Worship to be?

The Catholic's have a motto that says, *"The Mass never ends."* Should worship end when we walk out of church on Sunday afternoon? Does our contemporary view of Worship embrace the same values as biblical worship?

To fully appreciate worship as God intended it, we must first consider the significance of its biblical and historical definition. The modern word for Worship has many different meanings.

Many authors like to use Webster's definition of worship: *extravagant respect or admiration for or devotion to an object to esteem (i.e. Worship God vs worship of money).* The true meaning of worship found in the New Testament is found in the Greek word *proskuneo* (pros-koo-neh'-o), which means to *kneel or prostrate before someone.* This word is found sixty times in the New Testament. From this word comes another Greek word, *proskunetes* (pros-koo-nay-tace') which means *to fall upon the knees and touch the ground with the forehead as an expression of profound reverence.* A true worshipper therefore is one who falls down in reverence to God. John 4:23 explains what a worshipper is: "Yet a time is coming and has now come when the true *worshipers* will worship the Father in spirit and truth, for they are the kind of worshipers the Father seeks," (emphasis added). God is certainly worthy of our respect, admiration, and devotion. But I wonder how many Christians are willing to expend energy to truly worship God.

A typical church in today's culture has a Minister of Worship, or a designated person to "lead worship." Today, it is universally accepted to describe the event that a Christian attends on Sunday as a 'worship' service. However, worship is not an event, it is a lifestyle.

CONTEMPORARY WORSHIP

The contemporary concept of worship is confined to a specific day, time, and place. Biblical worship is expressed as an expenditure of physical energy, as a covenant commitment, and more importantly, as a way of life. Contemporary worship seems to be committed to a momentary involvement, rather than engaging in a disciplined practice of abiding worship.

A niche has been created for Cultural Worshipologists:[1] 'experts', who respond to the controversial problems associated with postmodern worship, usually restricted to the programming of church services. Most Cultural Worshipologists are authors who discuss and offer advice on the most effective methods of conducting an efficient, relevant Sunday morning service.

The scriptural acts of worship such as meditating, waiting, and seeking involves the expenditure of energy. However, the focus of the Cultural Worshipologist is the dynamics and clarification of the worship event, time, place, and action. The act of Worship is intended to be a way of life not a once-a-week experience.

ALTERNATIVE WORSHIP

Looking for a new avenue of worship, the Baby Boomers, Generation X'ers, and Nexters are actively seeking a fulfilled experience that will grant them serenity. With the advent of the New Age movement, many disenfranchised Boom-X-Nexters began exploring new territory in search for the spiritual contentment they longed for. Many religious and New Age seminars and retreats are popping up all over the world like Plum Village in France, an idyllic Buddhist community where many Westerners are flocking to in search of inner peace. The retreat from mainstream religion is

1. Source: Author.

quickly causing a spike in conversions to alternative religious movements.

De-frocked Catholic Priest, Matthew Fox has created a sensation in San Francisco with his Techno Cosmic Mass, a religious experience ". . . that blends Western liturgical tradition with ecstatic music and dance, urban shamanism, multimedia imagery, and Eastern and indigenous spiritual elements . . . This tendency to mix elements of different traditions into new hybrid forms will continue in the new millennium, as seekers separated from their religious heritage search out new expressions of faith . . ."[2]

CHURCH LOYALTY

Loyalty to a given church or denomination is not as strong as it was forty or fifty years ago. This phenomenon has changed the definition of worship in our culture. Countless Americans are searching for a religious experience that will fulfill the gnawing pains of financial, relational, and emotional despair. Shopping for that fulfillment has opened new opportunities for churches to reach out and meet the unmet needs of these seekers. This ideology is the foundation for Sunday morning services set aside, for what is now the definitive term for worship. The Cultural Worshipologists of our day identify the need for worship services and define the style, typology, and operation of how to conduct a successful service.

The longing for a new way to worship plagued Baby Boomers for years. They quickly became dissatisfied with their "daddy's church" and decided to completely stop attend-

2. Cimino and Lattin, *Shopping For Faith*, 25–26.

ing. The old adage: This isn't your dad's Oldsmobile, seemed to hit home when it came to church attendance. A sudden hermeneutical paradox occurred during the late 1980s and early 90s. Disgruntled Boomers began to justify their lack of church attendance by rationalizing Jesus words found in John 4:21, 23, ". . . a time is coming when you will worship the Father neither on this mountain nor in Jerusalem . . . Yet a time is coming and has now come when the true worshipers will worship the Father in spirit and truth, for they are the kind of worshipers the Father seeks . . ."

Why should it matter where they worshipped? The justification of worshipping God in the woods during the height of hunting season seems innocently rational. Like the predecessors before them, Generation X'ers, and the Nexters generations want instant spirituality.

The concern for many churches today is to redirect their focus from a generation of parishioners who survived the Great Depression, to a generation that is depressed. This is not to say they are ignoring an aging generation, but the spotlight is now shining on the youth of its members.

Growing up in a world of entertain me and I-Want-It-Now, the Generation X'ers and the Nexters have been one of the hardest segments of our culture to reach. With this in mind churches are eager to find ways to meet the needs of these lost generations. The combination of contemporary music, drama, and reasonably timed sermons, as a new form of worship, brought many back to the local churches.

Are we moving away from our biblical roots towards a market driven, consumer minded way of doing worship? The Corporate Worshipper of the 21st Century has shifted the method of worship from participant to spectator. Many churches today are programming services to be held on Sunday and polishing it with slick, accurately timed music, and packaging it as "worship." Many would question why this is a bad thing. Why should we stifle our creative energies to bring souls through the doors into our churches, isn't this what we're supposed to do? Is it wrong to have a beautiful building? Is it a sin to have effective programming?

The question isn't where we meet, how we meet, or how effective the meeting is. What we should consider is the purpose of meeting together. The early church met as one body (Acts 2) and went out into the world. Shouldn't we be asking, "Are we doing what the early church did?"

A close look at how change has affected our cultural thoughts is to look at the magnificence of God's hand at work, evidenced by historical events that shaped how we once worshipped. As early as four decades ago, revivals greatly affected Christendom and the way we approach worship.

THE ASBURY REVIVAL

The Asbury Revival of 1970 simply started when Custer Reynolds, Academic Dean, and speaker for this particular service on February 3, 1970, stepped out of his programmed sermon and asked students to spontaneously give their testimony. What transpired was one of greatest revivals of the 1900's. A simple act of obedience changed the lives of thousands. From this revival, other revivals spread throughout the country due to students fanning out and spreading the Word of God and word of this miraculous event that was taking place.

The service at the great Asbury College Revival (1970) started as a scheduled (programmed) Chapel Service for 50 minutes in Hughes auditorium. One hundred and eighty-five continuous hours later it was showing signs of slowing down. One student reported coming into the auditorium hours after the Revival hit, and thought he had been sitting for 20 minutes. When he looked at his watch, to his disbelief, he had been sitting in Hughes auditorium for nearly six hours! People did not want to leave. Reconciliation, healing, and salvation were simultaneously occurring throughout this miraculous event.

One particular revival happened at the Meridian Street Church of God in Anderson, Indiana. Several students (from Asbury) were asked to come and give their testimonies. What happened next was a spontaneous revival that lasted 50 consecutive nights.[3] What would happen if we freed ourselves to let the Holy Spirit move like Custer Reynolds did? Revival occurs when hungry hearts come before God in anticipation. Hungry hearts are an outcome of lifestyle worshippers.

CONTEMPORARY METHODOLOGY OF WORSHIP

Worship today is defined by the *Method of Creation*[4] (hereafter MOC): the method of *creating* a worship service. Culturally driven worship is now prepared, practiced, and produced. A systematic process or methodology is used to create a worship experience. Songs, and/or, dramatic acts/

3. *Lexington-Herald*, "A Revival Account Asbury 1970," May 2008.
4. Source: Author.

liturgy, are prepared in advance of the Christian event, known as: Worship. After the events are prepared, a specific date, time, and place are utilized to practice. With final preparations in place, the production is presented at the appointed time, at the appointed place, on the appointed date.

Many mainstream Evangelical churches have utilized the Vineyard's approach to the MOC, also known as the Wimber Five-Phase Model, named after Vineyard founder, John Wimber. This model is broken into five phases using Psalm 95 as reference; each phase is a type or group of songs engineered for its specific purpose:

1. Invitation Phase—Upbeat songs used to aid the participant in a call to 'worship'.

2. Engagement Phase—Slower songs that entice participants to draw closer to God.

3. Adoration Phase—More subdued songs asking the participants to focus their attention on God.

4. Intimacy Phase—Slow songs allowing the participant to 'lose' themselves in the music while praising and worshipping God.

5. Closeout Phase—Transitional songs that move the participant out of the Intimacy phase to the next segment of 'church'.

This MOC is the most widely accepted vehicle for participants to experience worship and has now been practiced for the last two decades. Critics postulate a firm reasoning for the MOC as a reverent, organized, and ordained sacrament to God. God is definitely not the author of confusion, and does expect our acts to be done orderly. However, are we allowing God to be God? A.W. Tozer said, "If the Holy Spirit was withdrawn from the church today, 95 percent of what we do would go on and no one would know the difference. If the Holy Spirit had been withdrawn from the New Testament church, 95 percent of what they did would stop, and everybody would know the difference."

In the November 29, 2004 publication of the Barna Group, a survey entitled *Americans Describe Sources of Spiritual Fulfillment and Frustration*, discovered that "Less than one percent listed worshipping God as their means of fulfillment, and a similarly miniscule number claimed that leading someone to Christ was their major source of satisfaction."[5] The quintessential question is: "Why are worship services thriving and popular to the Evangelical masses, yet less than 1% are being fulfilled by worshipping God?" This research bolsters the argument that people are seeking worship experiences for the experience (like our fictitious character Kari), rather then seeking worship as outlined in the Bible, as a way of life.

Christians today, generally do not go to church to have a Prayer service once a week. Yet, prayer is an active part of our daily life. Wouldn't it would seem odd to go to church just to pray and then not pray again until the following Sunday? The attitude of our day is to wait until Sunday to go and worship God.

There is no question that there is a hunger for spiritual fulfillment in the world today. The method of meeting the needs of spiritual thirst and hunger is the position today's

---

5. Barna, "Americans Describe Sources of Spiritual Fulfillment and Frustration," para 3.

churches face. Should we be looking at the relevancy of programming services or re-examining the true worship of the Bible? Our contemporary attitude of worship should not be contradictive of biblical worship.

PRESENCE NOT PRESENTS

The recipients of Paul's letter to the Romans understood the concept of offerings. The act of offerings to a god was a common occurrence in the Greek and Roman culture. However, Paul's urging has more to do with whole commitment to God. The early believers didn't separate worship from their daily life. They wouldn't understand going to church on Sunday to worship. There was no distinction between public worship and private actions. Whether in private or public, worship was not delineated by time or geography, daily lifestyle was an act of worship. It would seem unnatural to them to spend 30–45 minutes in communal worship and then suddenly stop because a sermon or special music was expected. To the early believers, worship was a part of life just as breathing, eating, and sleeping.

Worship throughout the Bible is often about sacrifice. The meaning of Romans 12:1 to *offer your bodies* is to *present yourself to God*. The definitions also mean to *place at God's disposal* (or Will), and to bring into *fellowship or intimacy with God*. Paul was speaking from the point of someone who didn't separate worship from lifestyle. Worshipping meant denying sinful desires and finding intimacy with God, 24/7.

The Greek word for *bodies* found in Romans 12:1 is, *Soma,* which can mean either the dead body of a corpse, or a living body. Paul carefully makes the distinction that unlike sacrifices that are offered by Temple Priests, we as Priests bring (put at God's disposal) our living, breathing bodies before him daily.

COMMUNAL WORSHIP

Corporate worship is defined today by what we know as culturally significant. Although cultural flashpoints are relevant for biblical review, misguided characterizations of these cultural practices are more commonplace today. Recognition of cultural needs is paramount to church leaders in our postmodern society. However, blending cultural practices and beliefs within a biblical framework is a misguided effort to grow churches and satisfy the appetites.

A more appropriate term for believers meeting together to worship is "communal." Although semantical in nature, the postmodern church incorrectly titles this event "corporate worship." The term "communal worship" implies a more personal kinship with fellow participants. Corporate worship, although linguistically correct, synchronizes the assembly of acquaintances at a physical site on a given day.

The decisive nature of corporate assemblage is to create an environment that often caters to a specific audience. Cultural Worshipologists have introduced "blending", using old hymns along with contemporary choruses in a worship service, therefore meeting the needs of both young and old. The current trend in corporate assemblage has moved from choirs to worship teams creating an orchestrated effort to make the musical aspect of worship more interactive.

Assembly is critical for encouragement, exhortation, and discovery. However, the temperament of the contemporary church is fixated on time-table-worship. The early church was fixated on lifestyle worship.

When the early Believers met together (as seen in Acts 2 & 4), they met with the attitude of Faith. How many churches or church members today would give up their building funds to help the poor? This is the act of worship the early believers committed themselves to. They didn't comprehend their personal finances being separate from worship. They were at God's disposal.

The early church was centered on God and what He was saying. God expects order in our lives and in our communal gatherings. However, the early church didn't program him out of their gatherings.

EARLY ACTS OF WORSHIP

Did you ever stop to think of how the early church was able to feed the hungry, care for the orphans and widows, and those struggling financially? Was a committee in charge of this social service? In the book of Acts we find numerous passages that declare how the believers were of one accord, or one mind (Acts 1:14, 2:1, 2:46, 4:24, 5:12, 8:6, 1:25). In Philippians (2:1–5) we find Paul encouraging the early church to examine themselves and to come together as one, "If you have any encouragement from being *united* with Christ, if any comfort from his love, if any fellowship with the Spirit, if any tenderness and compassion, then make my joy complete by being *like-minded*, having the same love, being *one in spirit* and *purpose*. Do nothing out of selfish ambition or vain conceit, but in humility consider others better than yourselves. Each of you should look not only to your own interests, but also to the interests of others." (emphasis added)

As individual worshippers, they met as a united body. Their like-minded attitudes came from individual acts of continued worship. The drive and determination to help those in need didn't come from a committee; they saw needs and acted. This was their *spiritual act of worship* found in Romans 12:1.

I have heard critics say that it was different then and times have changed. If the example of what the early believers did is included in God's Word, along with the Acts of the Apostles, and the life of Jesus, why is it different? What has changed? Has Faith taken a back seat to tightly programmed corporate gatherings?

Just for a moment, picture yourself in Heaven and look down at a church service through God's eyes? What is He thinking? His hand is always reaching out (Isaiah 50:2), his ear is waiting for our call (Isaiah 55:3, Matthew 10:27), and his voice is ever-present waiting for us to hear (Isaiah 28:23, Revelation 3:20). Are we able to experience God during our communal gatherings, or are we too focused on the programmed service to hear him? There is nothing wrong with an orderly service, but do we offer the opportunity for God to show up?

When Believers come together they worship as a Body. Whether it is a building or a group of Believers gathered on a beach, church is when people come together as God's Body to worship him unified. Personally, when you and

God meet, worship is created. Richard Foster says, ". . . we have not worshiped the Lord until spirit touches spirit."[6]

The opportunity for personal growth should be the focus of the local church. It is very disturbing to find that worship is now an event found in a Strategic Planning manual instead of an outward act of humble people. Isn't it interesting that C. Peter Wagner, the father of Church Growth Consulting, has shifted his energies from Church Growth to Prayer and Evangelism?

THE FEDORA-WEARIN'-BRIEFCASE-TOTIN' HANDYMAN

His neatly trimmed beard and fedora makes him look more like an accountant then a handyman. Instead of a tool belt, he carries a briefcase, filled with special tools. Tim certainly doesn't fit the image of your typical handyman. He lives in a small camper and seems very content with his life. He finds odd jobs to keep himself busy through the summer and works as a security guard at a nearby lake in the fall and winter.

Shortly after hurricane Katrina destroyed homes, cities, and businesses, Tim packed up his tools, got in his truck, and headed out from Nashville towards New Orleans. God spoke to Tim and told him to go. Without knowing what lay head, without knowing anyone, without hesitation he simply said, "Here am I, send me," and he went. The events that followed and the lives he touched were not broadcast on the evening news. He was not honored during a Sunday church service. He wasn't awarded a medal. He simply acted

---

6. Foster, *Prayer*, 158.

from his heart. Tim understands his *spiritual act of worship* (Romans 12:1), living by faith, living a *lifestyle* of worship. If only we all had the faith of Tim.

WHO'S IN CHARGE?

Is worship today defined by what happens on stage every Sunday? Do we see the outcome of our weekly lifestyle worship during our Communal gatherings? Is our local body a breeding ground for spiritual growth, or a weekly meeting of acquaintances?

The book of Acts pays tribute to the obedience of God's people assembled with a unity of spirit. The key to the second chapter of Acts is found in the last verse, last sentence (2:47), "And the *Lord* added to their number daily those who were being saved," (emphasis added). The previous verses describe how the worshippers were of one mind, a true 'body' of Christ. They lived and worshipped in a communal setting, serving one another.

Instead of creating a special program or forming a committee, they simply got on their knees and prayed (Acts 6:1–7). And it was *the Lord* that caused the church to grow. Not a growth campaign or special programs. It was the faith of the early believers that caused God to act. Faith derived from a lifestyle of worship.

The true sense of leadership in worship should be God who is alive and active in the presence of the community. How often is leadership clouded by the righteous indignation of an "organized" service, or how a forced sermon has magnificently quenched the Holy Spirit? God acts when his people humble themselves before him (2 Chronicles 7:14, Isaiah 66:2).

Revivals and miraculous meetings are the outcome of believers waiting for their Worship Leader to act. If faith is not an active ingredient of believers gathering together, then how can God act? It is only when believers who understand lifestyle worship, come together with other like-minded believers will God be allowed to lead.

PRAISE & WORSHIP

My Grandfather was a quick-witted Irishman who spent most of his life as a farmer in Northwestern Michigan. He taught me to find humor in life in the most unexpected places, yet it always came with a life lesson. I remember one time as a teenager I had the opportunity to spend the day alone with grandpa. We drove into town to pick up supplies for the farm. As we came into the city limits he noticed a sign and began to chuckle. "Do you see that sign there?" he asked, pointing to a sign that said, *Slow Children Playing*. "Yes," I said, looking at him quizzically. He began to chuckle louder, "I've never seen a child play *slow* in my entire life," he said as I watched his belly spasm with laughter.

To this day I am humored by signs and odd words that are put together. While living in Phoenix, Arizona, I was driving down the street and saw a sign that made me remember Grandpa McNeilly. It was Christmas time and makeshift tree lots could be found on vacant corner lots. As I approached a lot I saw a sign advertising the trees that read: *Live Christmas Trees For Sale*. All I could think of as I chuckled was, "As opposed to what, dead Christmas trees?"

We often try to make words and slogans alluring to attract people to our churches. Slick, snazzy phrases appeal to the cultural relevance of today's church. However, phrases like, *Praise* and *Worship* are redundant. We worship God through praise. It is like saying, "We pray and speak to God." Prayer *is* speaking to God. Worship *is* praising God. Reverence, adoration, thanksgiving, and respect are types of praise we offer to God through our act of worship.

These acts of Praise should be commonplace in our everyday lives. We shouldn't have a Praise & Worship service. We should have *intimate-encounter-with-God meetings*; an encounter, that reflects our continued growth through our daily worship of him.

HUMANISTIC-CHRISTIANITY

Humanistic-Christian values are permeating through the postmodern church. Our culture is now saturated with massive amounts of literature on the subject of how-to-do-worship. Authors, Pastors, Worship Leaders, and Musicians are attempting, within their own power, to create a worship experience (MOC).

The definition of Humanistic-Christianity is: *A Christian's attitude to seek, solve, pursue, and maintain life within individual parameters and power, void of faith.*[7] Independently these two words contradict each other. But the New Age Christian is replacing God with a do-it-myself doctrine: *instead of getting on our knees before God to seek*

7. Source: Author.

a pastor, let's hire a recruiting firm to hire our staff; *before we trust God to give us direction*, let's seek out a consulting firm to help us grow a church; *in lieu of Faith*, let's just do it ourselves.

Humanistic-Christian theology is sprouting throughout the contemporary church mindset. Churches, denominations, and pastors, who spend thousands of dollars to assist the physical growth of their church, prove the existence of Humanistic-Christian theology.

The justification for the existence of 'church growth' experts is evidence enough that Faith is not a factor in the personal (spiritual) growth of parishioners. Today Humanistic-Christian leaders are seeking to grow churches with external (physical world) assistance. Faith (spiritual world) seems to be an obsolete act performed by the Patriarchs of the past.

Contemporary views of the physical world and the spiritual world are oppositionally defiant. The Humanistic-Christian believes in a spiritual world in theory. The true Believer believes in a spiritual world in practice. To emphasize church growth is to accentuate quantity (physical world). The attitude of the postmodern church makes it difficult to talk about worship without discussing church growth. Without kneepads, the postmodern church must believe that inner growth will come by miraculous osmosis. Has faith become a theoretical term used only for historical and academic discussion?

THE MARY & MARTHA AFFECT

In Luke 10 we find two women who approach worship in two very distinct ways. Sisters Mary and Martha invited Jesus into their home, much like we do at church on Sundays. Martha had the mindset to be active for Jesus, to do everything in her physical power to make his visit a comfortable and memorable one. Her distraction to Jesus is analogous to the Humanistic-Christians who *do* for God. They create, plan, and execute without first sitting, listening, and obeying. Mary understood the concept of lifestyle worship. She knew that this appointed time, what we call "church", was a time for worship, so she stopped, and waited for Jesus. Martha's concept of "church" was to try and create an atmosphere of worship (MOC). Although she was doing what a good Hebrew woman was taught to do, Martha missed the opportunity to be in Jesus presence.

I often wondered why this story is included in the life of Jesus. I now believe it is to direct us to wait and listen to our Lord. Do we treat our communal gatherings as a time to be with our Lord, or do we hope He will show up after we have scurried around making everything just perfect for him, like Martha?

When we think of "serving" God, as related to Sunday worship, we conjure up thoughts of singing, praying, a sermon, offering, and other liturgy. The word for "worship" found in Romans 12:1 is *lateria, (lat-ri'-ah)* which means 'service,' to offer ourselves, our bodies as *living sacrifices* to God in whatever service, or manner He asks of us. Therefore, true service to God is sacrifice. However, for many, the concept of sacrifice may hold the same attitude that Martha had. The attitude God is looking for is Mary's; spending time in his presence.

The quandary our contemporary churches face is the strict vernacular expression used for worship. Worship as a lifestyle includes meeting with others who are seeking God. In his wonderful book, *Who Needs God,* Harold Kushner has this to say about worship, "It's not that we go to church or synagogue at a stipulated time because God keeps office hours. We go because that is when we know there will be other people there, seeking the same kind of encounter we are seeking . . . We go in thinking of ourselves as an audience, with the same anticipation we bring to the theatre . . . But we can't be passive spectators . . . Without active participation, it will not happen."[8]

Working together, communal assemblage should be a growth experience for the active participants (Proverbs 27:17). When we assemble communally we exercise our Spirit-bestowed gifts for each other's benefit; we encourage and exhort each other; and all grow together into Christ. This does not happen when we isolate ourselves from other believers.[9]

LET GOD BE GOD

Christians assemble together and worship individually in a communal setting. The gathering of Christians for specific causes can generate a life changing experience or cloak the true meaning of worship. God rejoices when we work together as one body. Individually, he exhorts us to raise holy

---

8. Kushner, Harold S. *Who Needs God,* 151.
9. Pinckney, Coty. "The Essence of Worship," para. 20.

hands in worship (1 Timothy 2:8), to clap (Isaiah 55:12), to sing (Psalm 30:4; 47:6), and to give ourselves fully in worship (Romans 12:1). Great and mighty events have happened when God's people come together. The second chapter found in the book of Acts pays tribute to the obedience of God's people assembled with a unity of spirit.

The key to the second chapter of Acts is found in the last verse, last sentence (2:47), "And the *Lord* added to their number daily those who were being saved," (emphasis added). It is only through Faith, not Humanistic-Christian endeavors, that God builds a church. The emphasis today is put on *added their numbers daily* instead of placing the glory where it should be . . . on the *Lord*.

The previous verses describe how the worshippers were of one mind, a true body of Christ. They lived and worshipped in a communal setting, serving one another. It wasn't a Consultant who showed how to increase the church. It wasn't a polished vocal performance. It was simply faith, and obedience, believing God would act, through an act of Worship.

2

Palmolive Prayers

WITH ZEAL and fervency we are to live effervescently for God. The Greek word for "living" is *Zao* (dzah'-o). The Greek word for "sacrifices" is *Thusia* (thoo-see'-ah). These two words seem contradictory when put together, "Therefore, I urge you, brothers, in view of God's mercy, to offer your bodies as *living sacrifices*, holy and pleasing to God—this is your spiritual act of worship" (Romans 12:1 emphasis added), but the New Covenant created by Jesus, does not require the offering of dead animals but rather living, breathing, holy believers to be ready and accountable before God.

WHY WORSHIP?

Why do we worship? The obvious answer is to give honor to God. The first commandment given to us declares that we are to worship God and no other gods (Exodus 20:1–3). He created us and desires that we recognize his existence and our inability to survive without him. The more intimate we are with him, the more we see and experience his majesty. But why do we need to worship together?

The purpose of meeting in a communal setting, as outlined in Hebrews 10:24–25, is for encouragement and accountability. Not one book in the New Testament uses the term worship for the act of corporate assemblage nor is there any precept regarding worship in communal gatherings. However, the New Testament is filled with the acts of lifestyle worship. The book of Acts is dedicated to the Apostles and other believers living a lifestyle of worship.

The Believers of the New Covenant understood that the body, soul, and spirit were united. Worship was, and still is, a way of life. They didn't separate worship from services or meetings. They didn't understand the concept of worship the way the postmodern church uses it to separate the Christian life with an event.

One distinction between contemporary worship and the assemblage of New Covenant believers was the expectation of all of the believers of the early church to actively participate at each meeting. Today, traditions are steeped in singing a few songs, announcements, a special song, the offertory, and the sermon, with little or no interaction between believers.

Communal Worship involves individuals participating in an intimate encounter with God. Individually they meet, together they focus on a single goal: to worship God. Worship is not a spectator event like a concert or football game. However, many corporate worshippers react to Sunday services as if it were an entertaining event. God isn't concerned about specific times and geographic places. He is concerned about the heart and attitudes of believers.

Lifestyle worship found in scripture transcends today's cultural notion that says, "I've been to church today, therefore I have done my duty and worshipped." It clearly defines worship as a consistent way of life. So, should we abandon our Sunday morning services for the sake of individual worship? Communal worship is not to be avoided, yet it is not to be the substitution for daily communion and intentional adoration to God.

BACK TO BASICS

In his wonderful book *The Unquenchable Worshipper*, Matt Redman shares his worship experiences with Mike Pilavachi, founder of Soul Survivor in Watford, England, who reconsidered the act of worship:[1]

"Mike, the pastor, decided on a pretty drastic course of action: We would strip everything away for a season, just to see where our hearts were. So the very next Sunday when we turned up at church, there was no sound system to be seen and no band to lead us. The new approach was simple: We weren't going to lean so hard on those outward things anymore."

It was Mike Pilavachi's fundamental belief that stripping away all facades and embracing God would stir the hearts at Soul Survivor. It didn't take a committee to allow this to happen. It occurred out of obedience. It was shortly after this experience that Matt wrote one of his most famous songs *The Heart of Worship*.

Showing up on Sunday, singing a few songs, and listening to a sermon is not lifestyle worship. Our participation on Sunday should not differ then what we do all week. The difference is we are rejoicing with other Believers. Sunday Services are often dessert for many in their Christian walk. However, Corporate Worship is becoming a sugar-fix for

1. Redman, *The Unquenchable Worshipper*, 103.

many without fully understanding the impact of what the *spiritual act of worship* (Romans 12:1) means in relationship to the Believer and God. When was the last time you heard a sermon on the *Prayer Involves Time* or *Give up T.V. for Prayer* or how about *Cancel Your Golf Game for God*? This is not something you would see on a church marquee.

Assembly has its place in the life of the believer, but the Lifestyle of worship is a daily, minute-by-minute way of life. Dr. David Peterson, one of the most respected New Testament Theologians of our time says that, ". . . people who emphasize that they are 'going to church to worship God' tend to disregard what the New Testament says about the purpose of the Christian assembly. If Christians are meant to worship God in every sphere of life, it cannot be worship as such that brings them to church."[2]

GROWING STRONG BELIEVERS

Lifestyle worship cannot be taught, practiced, or fully understood when the focus is on growing churches. Corporate worship is an outcome of aggregate management. Church leaders have discovered that managing a flock under the auspices of "corporate worship" is more simplified, and manageable than teaching and nurturing inner growth through personal development and discipleship.

Jesus used what business leaders today would call *micro management* to strengthen the church. He didn't command an audience of hundreds or thousands. He merely called twelve simple men to follow him, to learn,

---

2. Peterson, *Engaging With God, A Biblical Theology of Worship*, 219.

and to grow. The fraternities and rulers of the day were not concerned during the infant stages of his ministry. Twelve disciples were hardly a threat to these important leaders. They had throngs of followers to manage and did so with a corporate mentality. Jesus, on the other hand, knew that developing a small group of individuals would ultimately strengthen the church.

The contemporary church has created an atmosphere of client-centered worship. The day set aside for communal worship has been restricted to a one or two hour period of time. Within this time constraint a packaged program has been established and contains an interlude of thirty to forty-five minutes of music.

Corporate worship is defined today by what we know as culturally significant. Although cultural flashpoints are relevant for biblical review, misguided characterizations of these cultural practices are more commonplace today. Recognition of cultural needs is paramount to church leaders in our postmodern society. However, blending cultural practices and beliefs within a biblical framework is a misguided effort to grow churches and satisfy the appetites.

LORD OF THE DISHES!

Brother Lawrence, a Carmelite monk during the 1600s, was a lowly kitchen worker of the Discalced Carmelite in Paris. His uncanny approach to developing an intimate relationship with God is chronicled in *The Practice of the Presence of God*. Brother Lawrence found an incredible time of worship while washing dishes. It may be hard to fathom someone standing at a large sink, scrapping off plates of half-eaten meals, crying out, "Lord of all pots and pans and things, make me a saint by getting meals and washing up the plates," but such was Brother Lawrence.

At first he despised his job as a lowly kitchen worker. But he began to realize that God was alive in everything he did no matter how frivolous or humbling it may be. He found a moment-to-moment, second-to-second encounter with God. In the midst of dirt, grime, chaos, and humbling labor, he found the true meaning of lifestyle worship.

The true calling of a Christian is to live in the ordinary but realize that through lifestyle worship life becomes extraordinary. Life may, at times, be difficult, but the next time your hands are soaking in Palmolive dish soap, remember that God is *Lord of all pots and pans and things*.

HEAVENLY WORSHIP

If we are unable to devote our lives to worship, how do we think we will survive in heaven when worship is an ongoing, eternal experience? What can we learn from worship in heaven? A close look at the Old and New Testament opens a wonderful window into what we can look forward to when we see God face to face. We find heavenly beings praising God day and night.

In the Old Testament, Nehemiah shares with us that the *multitudes* of heaven worship God, "You alone are the LORD. You made the *heavens*, even the highest *heavens*, and all their starry host, the earth and all that is on it, the seas and all that is in them. You give life to everything, and the multitudes of *heaven worship* you" (Nehemiah 9:6, emphasis added). In Isaiah 6:1–3, we read that in his vision he sees ". . . the Lord seated on a throne, high and exalted, the train of his robe filled the temple. Above him were seraphs, each with six wings: With two wings they covered their faces, with two they covered their feet, and with two they were flying. And they were calling to one another: 'Holy, holy, holy is the Lord Almighty; the whole earth is full of his glory."

The book of Revelation gives us a deeper insight of what heavenly worship is all about. In Chapter 4 we see twenty-four Elders falling down, crying out to God, "You are worthy, our lord and God, to receive glory and honor and power, for you created all things, and by your will they were created and have their being" (4:10–11). In verses 11:16, 17, we discover they each have their own seat that surrounds the throne of God.

The Elders, persons of honor, leave their seats of prestige, stand up, take notice and fall down in humble submission to God. They not only lie down and prostrate themselves, but they throw their gold crowns at the feet of God. The word for throw or "cast" is the Greek word *ballo* (bal'-lo), which has the meaning of *throwing something without caring where it falls*, and *to give over to one's care uncertain about the result*. A modern example of the incredible act of worship by the Elders, might be the same as a wealthy man taking his wealth and giving it all away and offering himself to God without a second thought to his intentions. The Elders gave their most prized possessions without question, and fell prostrate in loving reverence and honor to God. The heart of lifestyle worship begins with the attitude of complete surrender to God.

Would it seem unbelievable to go to church on Sunday morning and see your elders, deacons, or trustees falling prostrate? And for the congregation to spend the entire morning just giving praise to God? This is what is happening in heaven. If we are unwilling to fall down, cry, shout, and sing to God now, how will we be ready to do it when we meet him in heaven? Our 24/7, dimensional understanding makes it somewhat difficult to grasp the full magnitude of what is happening here. The Elders are our role models for offering our bodies as *living sacrifices*.

If this is a snapshot of how worship is practiced in Heaven, shouldn't we be doing it here on Earth? Worship is a physical, mental, spiritual, emotional, and sacrificial expression. It is the totality of our existence. The true acts of worship are found in the whole of our being causing us to live out a lifestyle of worship.

HORIZONTAL OR VERTICAL WORSHIP?

The phenomenon today is the rush to quantitatively grow churches. Church Growth experts are not concerned about the quality of personal growth; rather they are fixated on numbers, which sadly church leaders use to reflect their success or failure. Although, "programs" of nominal value are key ingredients to their master plan, the ultimate goal is to pad the pews with more parishioners.

From an economic standpoint, the industry of Church Growth has spawned the creation of a niche market. Numerous companies are reaping the benefits of aggressive denominations looking to fill their pews. Many church leaders myopically view Church Growth consultants as a tool to reach the lost. Some would argue that consultants are equipping church leadership (pastors) with information to better minister to the corporate worshipper. Others view these consultants as money-mongers of christian consumerism.

The buzzword among Church Growth consultants today is Healthy Church. Most critics find this to be nothing more than a marketing ploy. The common creed of contemporary churches seems to be forget about discipleship and bring on the masses.

GROWING OBESE CHURCHES

One Church Growth consultant boasts of doubling classes (Sunday school, small groups, etc.) every two years. Evangelism is certainly a posturing factor in the life of Christians. However, the objective to "double classes" every two years is not an emphasis Jesus taught. Author Os Guinness notes:

> One Christian advertising agent, who both represented the Coca Cola Corporation and engineered the *I Found It* evangelistic campaign, stated the point brazenly: "Back in Jerusalem where the church started, God performed a miracle there on the day of Pentecost. They didn't have the benefits of buttons and media, so God had to do a little supernatural work there. But today, with our technology, we have available to us the opportunity to create the same kind of interest in a secular society." Put simply, another church-growth consultant claims five to ten million baby boomers would be back in the fold

within a month if churches adopted three simple changes: (1) advertise; (2) let people know about product benefits; and (3) be nice to new people.[3]

The numerical expansion of a local church is inconsistent with Jesus's teaching. He was not concerned with trendy influences of temple worship. His motivation was for believers to depart from the religious masquerade and draw nearer to God. The opportunity to make a living within the church is not a questionable offense in itself. However, the concept of corporate worship as a duplicative method, used for financial gain, is problematic. Growing obese churches is not the answer for growing strong Christians.

The sad reality is that we are witnessing a market-based approach to increasing church growth in our contemporary Christian culture. Like it or not, we are faced with a marketplace of spirituality. The attitude of come, see, taste, and feel how good we are resonates through the sanctuaries of churches eager to pull in seekers.

SELLING GOD

Jesus not only separated himself from the popular religious fraternities such as the Pharisees and Sadducees, but he also completely rejected the lifestyle of the sect of teachers known as Sophists. These learned men sold their scholarly knowledge, or *Sophia*, which means *wisdom*, to wealthy families. Often, they would use their debating skills to publicly showcase their trade. As marketable philosophers, they could make a comfortable living selling their intellectual services.

3. Guiness, "Sounding Out the Idols of Church Growth," para 35.

Jesus did not conform to the trends of the Sophist, Pharisees, Sadducees, or any other sect. He did not request money for his public or private teachings. He lived by faith. His popularity as an itinerant philosopher, who sought no compensation for his dispensation of *Sophia,* fueled the ire of jealous fraternities.

THE TRUE WORSHIP LEADER

There should be no disparity between Christian worship and biblical worship. If spiritual growth would become an outcome of true worship we would see strong, exciting churches springing up. Not obese churches that have grown through multiplication.

The opportunity for personal Christian growth should be the focus of the church. Has the postmodern church lost sight of individual growth? The church is comprised of individuals with specific needs. The analogy of looking at a forest (the church) and missing the beauty and attention of the individual trees (parishioners) is appropriate for assessing the vision of Church Growth consultants.

The motive of these entrepreneurs is to enlarge the forest regardless of the health of the trees. The nature of this concept is widely accepted in the postmodern church. A quick Google search shows that there are nearly one million *more* websites for Church Growth consultants than for Christian growth. The true worship leader should be someone who is directing and teaching people how to worship God continually.

HOLISTIC WORSHIP

The word holistic means, "... *relating to or concerned with wholes or with complete systems rather than with the analysis of, treatment of, or dissection into part . . .*"[4] Our contemporary characterization of worship separates (dissects) who we are with what we do. For example, we say we are going to a worship service *to worship*. If we aren't worshipping God daily we aren't being the true worshipper (*proskunetes*) God calls us to be. Cultural Worshipologists enjoy analyzing and treating worship services.

The Old Testament Hebrew believers understood worship as totality versus separation. Their understanding of Yahweh was to respond to him with their total being. Separating who they were from who Yahweh is was not a concept they could comprehend. They fully understood the integration of the whole person and worshipping Yahweh. This is holistic, or Lifestyle worship. Andrew Hill offers this explanation of Holistic Worship, "Hebrew worship in the Old Testament was participatory. Their synthetic understanding of the nature and constitution of the human being demanded that the whole person respond to Yahweh in worship, not just the spirit and soul."[5]

Whether in private or public, Hebrew worship was never delineated by time or geography. The Hebrew (and Greek) thought of worship was totality, rather than separation of worship from the man (or woman).

The behavior and understanding of contemporary worship is the meeting, singing, sermon-listening, fellow-

---

4. Merriam-Webster Online Dictionary, 2008, s.v. "Holistic."
5. Hill, *Enter His Courts With Praise!*, 110.

ship, and exiting a building on Sunday mornings. Critics may find this harsh and cold, but Cultural Worshipologists define and re-define this ritual. The fundamental differences are the heart and attitude of the participant. Dr. LaMar Boschman, author, speaker, songwriter, and president of the Worship Institute in Bedford, TX, comments, "While it may be true that God manifests His presence more in places dedicated to worship, it is also that He is everywhere. He is not more present in a church or on top of a mountain than He is in any other place. He is everywhere always . . . God is present in church. He is present in the grocery store. He is in your home. He is in the office. He is in the park. He is present everywhere. No boundaries can be ascribed to Him."[6]

Limiting worship to a building is limiting God's omnipresence. Does this give license to shut the doors of every church every Sunday morning? On the contrary, we should rejoice at every opportunity to meet with fellow believers and encourage one another.

Does this mean that the majority of churches in the world are not worshipping when they meet on Sunday morning? As mentioned in earlier chapters in Hebrews, the writer thus spurs us on to meet with other believers (Hebrews 10: 24–25). Are we more concerned with horizontal worship than opening our hearts in vertical worship? According to George Barna of the Barna Research Group, most Christians do not believe they have experienced the presence of God in the past year and have no plan for spiritual advancement and are not exerting much effort to grow

6. Boschman, *A Passion For His Presence*, 10.

in their faith.[7] With the increasing emphasis on *worship leaders* and *worship teams*, why isn't the power of God more manifest in the lives of Christians? The call to attention is the thirty minutes given to the postmodern definition of worship.

WORSHIP OF THE EARLY CHURCH

Believers of the early church engaged in meeting in homes, above shops, and sometimes in cemeteries. As the church enlarged they often removed walls in the home or broke into smaller groups. The organization of the early church was somewhat different than churches of today. Within the structure of the communal worship in the early church we find more congregational participation.

The early church didn't have the luxury of PowerPoint presentations to remember key points of a sermon or aid in corporate worship. Repetition of songs, scripture, and liturgical recitation were methods developed to aid the participant in memorization. The educational system at this time was a catechistic approach utilizing ancient texts and assessing the student on the ability of recitation. The spoken word was the standardized method of passing history, culture, and scripture from generation to generation.

The mindset of the early church was not to meet in a corporate worship setting but to meet as a community. Communal meals were a part of the experience, similar to our church potlucks. The emphasis on communal worship was the involvement of everyone in the specific community.

---

7. Barna, "Americans Describe Sources of Spiritual Fulfillment and Frustration," para 17.

A wonderful model of communal worship is found in Acts 2: 44–47 and 4:32–37:

> All the believers were together and had everything in common. Selling their possessions and goods, they gave to anyone as he had need. Every day they continued to meet together in the temple courts. They broke bread in their homes and ate together with glad and sincere hearts, praising God and enjoying the favor of all the people. And the Lord added to their number daily those who were being saved . . . All the believers were one in heart and mind. No one claimed that any of his possessions was his own, but they shared everything they had. With great power the apostles continued to testify to the resurrection of the Lord Jesus, and much grace was upon them all. There were no needy persons among them. For from time to time those who owned lands or houses sold them, brought the money from the sales, and put it at the apostles' feet, and it was distributed to anyone as he had need.

Can you imagine selling your home and bringing the profit you made and giving it all to God? Because of their obedience God *added to their number daily those who were being saved*. They were not concerned about mission statements or long-term planning. Their focus was serving God and meeting the needs of the community. The communal worshipper of the early church understood the *spiritual* act of worship, the act of giving of themselves as a *living sacrifice* (Romans 12:1). Almost in the same breath Paul makes a punctuated segue from personal worship to communal worship in Romans 12:4–6 saying, "Just as each of us has one body with many members, and these members do not have the same function, so in Christ we who are many form one body, and each member belongs to all the others. We have different gifts, according to the grace given us."

The practice of open communal worship reverted to temple worship when Constantine converted to Christianity in 312 C.E. He began to erect buildings so Christians could gather to worship. However, when these temples were built, pagan practices were incorporated into the worship experience. A few short decades later, the free act of temple worship was replaced with a programmed, ritualistic order of worship. Active participants became solemn spectators. The age of participation was gone; replaced with Humanistic-Christian values.

An examination of the evolutionary change of the early church provides an analogous scenario to the postmodern church. The disparity found here is the commitment of early believers to sanctify their hearts and mind to God. Publicity was not an option considered for expanding churches. Individual growth was the motivating force behind Paul's instruction. The words of the late Dr. Robert Webber are of prophetic warning, "Part of the problem is that we have made our churches into centers of evangelism and instruction. The focus of our services is on man and his needs instead of God and His glory. This is true, for example in music, where its triteness in content and tune tends to entertain rather than provoke worship. Further, a fancy pulpiteering has made worship seem peripheral or at least preliminary to preaching."[8]

8. Webber, "Worship (Part 1)," para 46.

You've probably heard the old adage: "Going to church doesn't make you a Christian anymore than going to your garage makes you an automobile." As a Christian, you don't go to church to *be* a Christian; a Christian is who you are. Worshipping God is what we do, or should be doing. It should be a way of life for us, not a stopping place fifty-two times a year.

To meet at a given, geographical site, and to be in *one accord*, doesn't happen by chance. A great example is found in the book of Acts. Acts 1:14 and 2:1 states that the believers were of *one accord* (King James Version) or *together* (NIV). The Greek word for *one accord* or *together* is *homothymadon* (*ho-mo-thü-mä-do'n*), which simply means, *with one mind, with one accord, with one passion*. It is used twelve times in the New Testament, ten of those times in the book of Acts. It is actually a compound word that means: *to rush along, in unison*. It gives us the visual of people rushing in to be together and worship God as one. The Message Bible interprets Acts 1:14 this way, "They agreed they were in this for good, completely together in prayer." Communal worship is meant to be a place where holistic, like-minded believers gather to worship God.

Our contemporary church may in part, utilize the biblical acts of worship. However, the differentiating factor is lifestyle worship versus geographic and timeline worship. The persecution of the early church understood Paul's words regarding lifestyle worship, ". . . offer your bodies as living sacrifices, holy and pleasing to God . . ." (Romans 12:1). Should we hire consultants to do our work, or imitate the acts of the early Christians and live by faith? Communal worship should reflect our personal lifestyle worship.

3

The Act of Worship

> *"Yet a time is coming and has now come when the true worshipers will worship the Father in spirit and truth, for they are the kind of worshipers the Father seeks. God is spirit and his worshipers must worship in spirit and in truth,"* (John 4:23–24).

THE FIRST commandment from God is to worship him. God spoke and said, "I am the LORD your God, who brought you out of Egypt, out of the land of slavery. You shall have no other gods before me," (Exodus 20:1–3). Throughout scripture we are encouraged to walk, follow, listen, and love God with our whole heart (Deuteronomy 10:12; 19:9; 30:20; Matthew 22:37). Our whole heart is our whole being. However, the postmodern church is culturally bound to the contemporary definition of worship. This linguistic juxtaposition creates a climate of mediocrity. In Isaiah God remarks that, "These people come near to me with their mouth and honor me with their lips, but their hearts are far from me. Their worship of me is made up only of rules taught by men" (Isaiah 29:13), which shows how mediocrity has lead to false faith.

Has the church strayed from its biblical foundations or improved on ancient traditions? Maybe we should take heed to Amos's admonition, "I hate, I reject your Festivals. Nor do I delight in your solemn assemblies. Even though you offer up to Me Burnt Offerings and your Grain Offerings, I will not accept them. And I will not even look at the Peace Offerings of your fatlings. Take away from Me the noise of your songs. I will not even listen to the sound of your harps. But let justice roll down like rivers. And righteousness like an ever-flowing stream," (Amos 5:21–24). The plague of indifference between history and marketable worship is the ability to distinguish between the motives of the heart, God's will and eternal intention. The act of lifestyle worship is an individual experience. It is the meeting of the supernatural with the natural.

THIS ISN'T YOUR DADDY'S CHURCH

As we look at history we can see the big picture of God's hand at work through the millennia in snapshots of time and how paradigm shifts through the centuries affected Christendom. These great paradigm shifts transformed new thoughts that evolved into exciting flashpoints of God's miraculous work. The Protestant Reformation put into action by Martin Luther changed the landscape of Christianity. The great evangelists of the early 1900s like Smith Wigglesworth, Frank Bartleman, Billy Sunday, and E. Stanley Jones, to name a few, had an amazing impact on the world. The great fervor of these great evangelists changed millions of lives. The great Asbury Revival of 1970 created a ripple effect with Evangelical Christians that has lasted decades. Woodstock-type music festivals have popped up all over the world because of God's work at the Asbury Revival.

Social Ecologist and Management guru Peter Drucker weighs in with his comments about historical flashpoints saying, "Every few hundred years in Western history there occurs a sharp transformation . . . Within a few short decades, society rearranges itself—it's worldview; its basic values: its social and political structures; its arts; its key institutions. Fifty years later, there is a new world. And the people born then cannot even imagine the world in which their grandparents lived . . . We are currently living through just such a transformation. It is creating the post-capitalist society . . ."[1]

During the latter part of the last century we were faced with an unusual war: the worship wars. It has continued to taunt us for many years. New thoughts on how we *do* church are still creeping into mainstream evangelical thought. Disillusioned with traditional approaches to worship many leaders are turning to active practices of movements like the Emerging or Emergent Church, and the Open Church. These movements are the outcome of skepticism towards the consumer driven approach to worship and the nonchalant attitude of justifying cultural practices as biblical directives. There are many new movements currently in action throughout the world such as Meta-Church, Cell Church, Covenant and International Communities, Home School movement, and Servant Evangelism. However, the reason for singling out the Open Church and the Emerging Church movements is their emphasis on change and restoring the heart of the early Christian church.

1. Drucker, *Post-Capitalist Society*, 1.

A cursory look at the Open Church and the Emerging Church will give us a better understanding of what is happening in our Christian culture and the impact it has on Lifestyle Worship. If you could watch a parade from high atop a building so you were able see the beginning and end of the parade, you would be able to witness different events occurring throughout the procession. If we look at the big picture of what God has done in history we will discover that we are currently experiencing a new movement of God. I am not advocating or denouncing either of these movements. They are examined for their particular mass appeal to Christians.

The Open Church

One of the fastest and most unique movements in the world is the Open Church movement. The Open Church movement was founded by Author Jim Rutz and has the support of many Christian leaders such as Christian pollster George Barna, International House of Prayer (IHOP) Director and author Mike Bickle, and C. Peter Wagner. The basic concepts of the Open Church are:

- The Church needs to get back to the basics of the New Testament Church.
- That Christians must take a more active role in their local fellowships.
- Turn the Communal gatherings into *Participatory* gatherings rather than *Spectator* events.
- Create an environment that actually allows people to use their gifts.

- To close the gap of a Pastor-centered fellowship to an equitable Pastor-Parishioner Fellowship.[2]

The very basic tenets of the Open Church are to reclaim *three of the freedoms* of the Early Church: *pure worship, true sharing, and free ministry*. Communication/Mass Media consultant David Bradshaw identifies the Open Church movement quite succinctly on his website as ." . . a widespread movement with no central coordination. Open churches are full- fledged institutional congregations that allow body life in three ways . . . open worship, in which laymen are allowed to speak in praise; open sharing, in which laymen are allowed a wide range of interaction, prayer, confession, song, testimony, teaching, etc; and open ministry, in which gifts are used both inside and outside the church-in accordance with the Spirit's innovation, not just in conformity to existing programs. Strong leadership is developed while clergy are freed from the CEO straitjacket . . ."[3]

Although the Open Church movement has operational offices in Georgia, it is not a denomination, rather it is a network of churches that share the same vision enabling the body of Christ to *be* the body of Christ (Romans 12:4–8). The emphasis is to call Christians back to the basics of biblical beliefs.

The Emerging Church

The Emerging Church describes the activity and events that are reshaping the way we do church. Its development

2. From The Open Church Ministries website http://www.openchurch.com.

3. http://www.myideafactory.net/bigpict.html.

stemmed from the following mix of a lack of growth in protestant churches, particularly amongst Generation X:

- Opposition to fundamentalist doctrines and practices in the modern church.
- A neglect of ancient Christian tradition and practices.
- Increasing suspicion of the missiology of the market-driven Mega-church and institutionalized Christianity.

Characteristics of the Emerging Church include some or all of the following elements:

- Highly creative approaches to worship and spiritual reflection, as compared to many American churches in recent years. This can involve everything from the use of contemporary music and films to liturgy or other more ancient customs.
- A minimalist and decentralized organizational structure.
- A flexible approach to theology whereby individual differences in belief and morality are accepted within reason.
- A holistic view of the role of the church in society. This can mean anything from greater emphasis on fellowship in the structure of the group to a higher degree of emphasis on social action, community building or Christian outreach.
- A desire to reanalyze the Bible against the context with the goal of revealing a multiplicity

of valid perspectives rather than a single valid interpretation.

- A continual re-examination of theology.
- A high value placed on creating communities built out of the creativity of those who are a part of each local body.[4]

In common with the House Church movement, the Emerging Church is challenging traditional notions of how the church should be organized. The frustration of stagnant, non-pliable traditional churches sparked a grass roots movement that has exploded throughout the world. There are no headquarters for the Emerging Church, but there is a very large following of closely-knit believers that unashamedly profess their allegiance to this new movement.

One of the key elements of the Emerging Church is its emphasis on deconstructing the traditional communal service and reconstructing it in a radical way. Often called alternative worship, many of these churches have effective methods to reach those that wouldn't otherwise attend a traditional Christian fellowship. The Emerging Church uses terms such as: *missional, re-defining, postmodern,* and *community* to objectify its purpose.

In keeping with the House movement that came on the scene a few decades ago, the Emerging Church is changing the concept of how the church should be structured or re-structured. The lack of centralization and non-doctrinal ecclesiology has actually benefited the Emerging Church movement. The basic elements of mutuality have created a phenomenon worldwide.

4. Definitions taken from various websites.

FLUID WORSHIP

New fellowships like Holy Joe's in London, England; Holy Disorder in Gloucestershire, England; ikon in Belfast, Ireland; Café Church and Small Boat Big Sea in Sidney, Australia; Solomon's Porch in Minneapolis, Minnesota; and Red in Chattanooga, Tennessee are all choosing to reconstruct communal worship with a radical approach. Many of these fellowships are experimenting with *Fluid Worship*. Fluid Worship is the utilization of unorthodox methods and mediums for worship during communal gatherings.[5]

Holy Joe's in London has been at the forefront of experimenting with Fluid Worship. With humble beginnings and humble hearts the community continues to pursue a street-level approach to church. They recognize that their communion service of lollipops and day-glo bubbles didn't work as they expected. However, they kept trying and after 20 years have developed an avant-garde approach that works. Their *meta::morphic* communal gathering service was designed to

."... remove anything between a person and God ... a large room or [marquee] would be filled with various 'stations' at which you might be expected to do something or watch something or pray something ... it was laid out like an art gallery and you interacted with whatever aspect appealed to you."[6]

At *Holy Disorder* located in Gloucestershire you may find disco lights, artificial smoke, poetry, and art when you visit

---

5. Term and Definition: Author.

6. http://www.holyjoes.com.

one of their services. As with most Emerging Churches, you will find interactive communal gatherings here. The Holy Disorder fellowship has a younger following. Many teens and young adults that generally would not attend any type of Christian gathering are seeking out Holy Disorder as a safe and non-threatening alternative to traditional church.

Small Boat Big Sea in Sydney is committed to developing relationships through communal activities. The temperate climate allows them to utilize outdoor activities for gatherings and evangelism. Keeping with the nautical theme they use B.E.L.L.S. to highlight their focus. They emphasize communal gatherings and lifestyle worship. The B.E.L.L.S. Communal gathering, which they call The Lounge, consists of:

- BLESS—as we gather we intentionally speak words of blessing and affirmation over each other.
- EAT—we eat a shared meal during which we break bread and drink wine to remember Christ's death for us.
- LISTEN—we provide a period for reflection, meditation, and listening to the voice of God.
- LEARN—we gather around the Scriptures and learn together, discussing issues that confront our world.
- SENT—one person each week shares about how they spend their week, how they image or shadow God in that context and the ways they sense God's calling in their daily work.

The B.E.L.L.S. daily worship, which they call Daily Examin, is a devotional to tune into lifestyle worship:

- BE in God's presence—bless God. Simply allow yourself to become aware of the presence of God surrounding you. Allow this presence to fill your entire being. Be in his presence.

- ENGAGE in a loving gaze at your day—really encounter it. Notice what happened—how you were in the day's events. Acknowledge where you experienced the touch of God. Acknowledge your failure to recognize God in this day. Entrust your day to the love, compassion, and mercy of God.

- LISTEN to God—allow God to speak to you about your day. Listen to how God wishes to respond to your day. Allow God the space and the silence to make known what is precious and necessary.

- LEARN from today—look to God. Look for ways to deepen your relationship with God in positive, life-giving and nourishing ways. Look to God for guidance.

- SINK into gratitude for God's presence in this day.[7]

The *Morph Community* based in Ipswich, England is an ever changing, "morphing" fellowship. Ironically, Morph is an offshoot of an Anglican Church (St. Matthew's) also located in Ipswich. Disillusioned with traditional church, leaders of Morph carefully worked with St. Matthew's to develop a fellowship for a younger generation. Although they have dotted-line accountability to St. Matthew's, they

7. http://www.smallboatbigsea.org.

are presenting a more liberal agenda than would be found in a traditional Anglican Church. On their website they offer the following vision:

- We seek to be open to new ways of worshipping God, we value being free to make mistakes as we experiment, and seek to provide a space where we are safe to explore our spirituality.

- We believe that God is active and present both in the world and in our worship, and expect to encounter him in both.

- We value the Bible as a unique revelation of God, and seek to engage with God's word and the issues that affect our world in a deeper way.

- We seek to make prayer a part of our life at every moment, part of what we are passionate about, part of our action.

- We value a wide range of ways of worshipping God using the Bible, music, liturgy, story, silence, culture, images, media, candles, symbols, and much more.[8]

Fluid worship services can be more sensory than the traditional church. In the traditional church you listen with your ears to hear a preacher's sermon or music from a choir. In Fluid Worship you may experience the touch of rough-hewn wood straddling a table to remind you of the rugged, harsh cross Jesus hung on. You may smell incense wafting through the room. You may see relevant artwork placed discreetly around you. You will hear interactive talk during

8. http://www.morphcommunity.org.uk.

what the modern church calls the "worship service." Some other unique changes you may see in Fluid Worship are:

- Worship Music. Worship teams play and sing from the back of the church putting more emphasis on the cross in the front.
- Worship Offering. Tables are set up in the front of the room or in a foyer off to the side with scriptures about worship on cards. Incense may be lit in remembrance that as we give our offering its scent goes up to God (Rev. 8:3–4; Ps. 141:2).
- Prayer Stations. Stations similar to a polling booth are set up around the room. Participants may go at any time into the Prayer Station and pray. Another option is to have tables draped with cloth. Candles and placards with different themes such as Family, Friendship, Finances, Personal, etc, with scripture by each and Bibles placed on the table. Participants are encouraged to go to the tables to pray and meditate.

There are multitudes of other methods used in Fluid Worship, which can change from Fellowship to Fellowship. Fluid Worship is created for the culture of the specific community. The use of disco lights and artificial smoke may not be as effective in conservative areas as it is with Holy Disorder in England. The focus of Fluid Worship is not simply on the music and art but the interactive and introspective nature of the early church; the *getting back to basics* and calling that is found in Scripture. The use of Fluid Worship is not proprietarily Protestant. Catholic, and as mentioned earlier, Anglican Churches are utilizing Fluid Worship in some form.

WORSHIP IN THE NEW MILLENNIUM

The behavior and understanding of contemporary worship is the meeting, singing, sermon-listening, fellowship, and exiting a building on Sunday mornings. The fundamental differences are the heart and attitude of the participant. The act of Worship is really, pre- and post-Sunday.

A careful review of worship found in Revelation does not reveal a programmed event. Spontaneous proclamations reverberate throughout Heaven. What would happen if the church opened its doors on Sunday morning and allowed every participant to fall, cry, shout, and sing to God? No bulletins, no announcements, no specials, no sermon, only God.

SOAKING

The book of Psalms gives homage to God through moods of lyrical declaration. Music is an inherent part of who we are as humans and we express ourselves musically through attitudes of emotion and devotion. The affect music plays on our being can carry us into a wonderful worship experience. The sad truth is that it is often interrupted by a programmed event, timed to meet the cultural needs of our society.

New full-length music services called Soaking are slowly spreading across the country. These services are designed to allow participants to focus on God in an interrupted environment. Kim and Alberto Rivera and Julie True are some the artists at the forefront of this new movement.

EXPRESSIONS

The mindset of the postmodern church wants believers to consider worship solely as a musical event, punctuated with emotional deliverance. However, music is not the only medium for worship. The following expressions confirm worship as a holistic act:[9]

- *Singing*: the book of Psalms, Ephesians 5:19, Colossians 3:16
- *Music*: 1st Chronicles 13:8, Psalm 33:3, Psalm 150
- *Clapping*: Psalm 47:1, Isaiah 55:12
- *Words*: Psalm 9:1, Psalm 73:28, Psalm 78:4–6
- *Laughing & Rejoicing*: Psalm 9:2, Psalm 126:1–3, Psalm 149:5, Zephaniah 3:14–17
- *Shouting*: Psalm 95:1, Psalm 98:4–6, Psalm 100:1
- *Silence*: Psalm 46:10, Habakkuk 2:20, Revelation 8:1
- *Standing*: 1st Chronicles 23:30, Psalm 24:3–6
- *Raising Our Hands*: Nehemiah 8:6, Psalm 63:3–5, Psalm 134:1–2, 1st Timothy 2:8
- *Bowing & Kneeling*: 2 Chronicles 7:3, Psalm 95:6, Daniel 6:10–11

---

9. This is a list in widespread use, and as with so much on the Internet the original author is unknown. This variant was found at www.xastanford.org.

- *Lying Prostrate*: Deuteronomy 9:18, Revelation 19:4
- *Leaping*: 2nd Samuel 6:16, Luke 6:23, Acts 3:7–8
- *Dancing*: Exodus 15:20–21, Psalm 149:3, Psalm 150:4

God does not limit how we worship him. Yet the actions of our contemporary church often stifle the joy and fullness of worship. Why do we continue to do church like we do it? Because that's the way we have been doing it for decades. It is comfortable. Have we considered Isaiah's words (29:13) and reflected on what we are really doing when we gather together? Are we really allowing God to be God?

The act of worship found in Romans 12:1 defines our actions as a true worshipper. The final three verses in the eleventh chapter of Romans (11:33–36) are known as the Doxology passage, "Oh, the depth of the riches of the wisdom and knowledge of God! How unsearchable his judgments, and his paths beyond tracing out! Who has known the mind of the Lord? Or who has been his counselor? Who has ever given to God, that God should repay him? For from him and through him and to him are all things. To him be the glory forever! Amen."

The next verse is Romans 12:1 where Paul emphatically declares, "*Therefore!*" Romans 12:1 could be Romans 11:37, a continuation of his thoughts on God's infinite wisdom and love for us. Here, Paul advocates for true personal worship, "Therefore, I urge you, brothers, in view of God's mercy (in reference to chapter 11:33–36), to offer your bodies as living sacrifices, holy and pleasing to God—this is your spiritual act of worship."

THE ACT OF WORSHIP

Scholars vary regarding the date the book of Romans was written but it is generally agreed that it was likely between 56–58 CE, and that Jesus' death and resurrection occurred somewhere between 27–36 CE. Therefore, about 20 years passed before Paul penned Romans. The early church went through many trials during these two decades and the mystique of Jesus as a sacrificial lamb wore off and became a reality. After establishing the principle of grace as our foundation for salvation, Paul continues instructing the believer in christian growth. The concept of a living sacrifice is no longer a foreign concept to grasp.

To fully appreciate the meaning of Romans 12:1, the dissection and interpretation of the words and their implications is necessary. The original documents, written in Greek, often lose significance in translation. Parsing the verse into the original meaning and significance offers credibility to the biblical act of worship: *"Therefore, I urge you, brothers, in view of God's mercy, to offer your bodies as living sacrifices, holy and pleasing to God—this is your spiritual act of worship."*

Therefore

>Greek Word: Oun
>Phonetic Spelling: oon
>Definition:
>
>1. therefore, these things being so.

Comment: As a reference to Romans 11:33–36, after contemplating on God, this word is an exclamation point, preparing the worshipper for this upcoming emphatic plea.

I *Urge* you

Greek Word: Parakaleo

Phonetic Spelling: par-ak-al-eh'-o

Definition:

1. to call to one's side, call for, summon
2. to address, speak to, (call to, call upon), which may be done in the way of exhortation, entreaty, comfort, instruction, etc.

Comment: The root word of *parakaleo* is *para* (par-ah) means: by, beside, or near. The word *kaleo* (kal-eh-o) has a strong reference to a very personal invitation to someone. It is to personally call out (loud) an invitation to come. Paul is personally, urgently, with respect, and encouragement calling believers to align their lives, as he has done, in accordance with God's amazing and awesome love for them.

Brothers

Greek Word: Adelfo or Adelfos

Phonetic Spelling: ad-el-fos

Definition/Comment: The word adelpo has the connotation of saying "siblings." It is not inherently used to call out to male listeners. In reality, it would be understood as "brothers and sisters." Paul is seeking a common ground for men as well as women to fully understand their responsibility to worship God, who in all of his majesty loves them equally.

in view of God's *Mercy*

> Greek Word: Oiktirmos
>
> Phonetic Spelling: oyk-tir-mos
>
> Definition:
>
>> 1. compassion, pity, mercy
>
> *Comment*: Paul emphasizes the Doxology (Romans 11) with his plea to the believer to understand God's grace and unfathomable compassion for them.

to *Offer* (more accurately translated: to *Present*)

> Greek Word: Paristemi
>
> Phonetic Spelling: par-is'-tay-mee
>
> Definition:
>
>> 1. to place beside or near
>> 2. to bring into one's fellowship or intimacy
>> 3. to stand beside, stand by or near, to be at hand, be present
>
> *Comment*: The emphasis is to be ready for and intimate with God. It is a call to come into an intimate fellowship with God.

your *Bodies*

> Greek Word: Soma
>
> Phonetic Spelling: so'-mah
>
> Definition:
>
>> 1. the body both of men or animals
>>
>>   a. a dead body or corpse
>>
>>   b. the living body

Comment: Although *Soma* could make reference to a dead, sacrificial animal, Paul adds 'your' bodies, and in the next breath speaks 'living sacrifice'.

as *Living*

Greek Word: Zao

Phonetic Spelling: dzah'-o

Definition:

1. to live, breathe, be among the living (not lifeless, not dead)
2. to enjoy real life
3. to have true life
4. to be in full vigour
5. to be fresh, strong, and efficient.

Comment: With zeal and fervency we are to live effervescently for God.

Sacrifices

Greek Word: Thusia

Phonetic Spelling: thoo-see'-ah

Definition:

1. a sacrifice, victim [sacrificial victim] (brackets mine).

Comments: The New Covenant between God and Man does not require the offering of dead animals; rather living, breathing, holy believers to be ready and present before God.

LIFESTYLE WORSHIP

Holy

> Greek Word: Hagios
>
> Phonetic Spelling: hag'-ee-os
>
> Definition:
>
> > 1. most holy thing, a saint
>
> *Comment*: Again Paul punctuates his exhortation with specific instruction. It is not just a living body we are to bring before God, but like the unblemished sheep brought as sin sacrifices, we are to bring our holy, living bodies before God. Some translations read, ." . . *a living and holy sacrifice . . .*"

and *Pleasing* (more accurately translated: *Acceptable*) to God

> Greek Word: Euarestos
>
> Phonetic Spelling: yoo-ar'-es-tos
>
> Definition:
>
> > 1. well pleasing, acceptable
>
> *Comment*: As each word or phrase builds on the next, we find that as we bring our physical bodies to God with an attitude of being a living sacrifice, we come into an acceptable union with God. We worship.

this is your *Spititual*

> Greek Word: Logikos
>
> Phonetic Spelling: log-ik-os'
>
> Definition:
>
> > 1. pertaining to the reason or logic
> >   a. spiritual, pertaining to the soul

b. agreeable to reason, following reason, reasonable, logical

Comment: The more widely known translation of 'spirit' is *Pneuma* (pnyoo'-mah). The specific translation for 'spiritual' found here in Romans 12:1 is the word *Logikos*. Paul has just finished his instruction on the grace and magnificence of God in Romans 11. With continued emphasis he logically calls us to wake up and realize that this is the reasonable way to worship God. Because of God's wonderful, infinite love for us, it just makes sense we should give him our entire being.

Act of Worship

Greek Word: Latreia

Phonetic Spelling: lat-ri'-ah

Definition:

1. service rendered for hire
2. any service or ministration: the service of God the service and worship of God according to the requirements of the Levitical law
3. to perform sacred services

Comment: Our sacred service (act of worship) is now to give our physical, spiritual, holistic self to God.

The Message Bible captures the heart of Romans 12:1, "Here's what I want you to do, God helping you: Take your everyday, ordinary life—your sleeping, eating, going-to-work, and walking-around life—and place it before God as an offering. Embracing what God does for you is the best thing you can do for him."

It is through meditation, silence, confession, and other acts of worship that we are able to renew our minds and come into an intimate relationship (worship) with God. Lifestyle worship is not a sedentary act. Christian Singer/Songwriter/Author Margaret Becker explains it this way,

"When we each seek our individual template for worship, we will be called to stand firm in places that others around us wouldn't-even though we are all part of the same body. This is never a popular or easy thing to do. But worship is like that—or at least it should be. If it doesn't require our best, it probably doesn't qualify as worship-not for a Holy God like the one we serve."[10]

LET'S GET PHYSICAL

The picture presented in Romans 12:1 is that of a Believer offering himself/herself to God through acts such as kneeling, lifting hands, prostrating, meditating, shouting, standing, clapping, dancing, singing, and waiting. Each of these acts requires a physical expenditure of energy. Even the acts of waiting and meditating necessitate the need to concentrate and focus.

In First Kings we find Solomon kneeling and lifting his hands. He physically knelt on the ground, raised his arms into the air, and prayed to God. After praying he stood (another worship act) and continued his worship by offering praise to God (1 Kings 8:54, 55). Ezra stood up and then fell to the ground with arms open wide and cried out to God (Ezra 9:5). Psalms 95:6 says, "Come, let us bow down in worship, let us *kneel* before the LORD our Maker," (empha-

10. Becker, *Coming Up For Air.*

sis added). As Michal watched David celebrating, she saw him dancing or literally, skipping and leaping (1 Chronicles 15:29). The Hebrew word for dancing is *raqad* (raw-kad), which means to skip about, to leap, and to dance. David was physically worshipping God with the heart of a child.

Each of these great men of God could have easily sat back and said a few prayers from the comfort of their plush surroundings. Instead they did what came naturally, they worshipped from their heart. It was not a foreign act; it came from their entire being. They lived a worship lifestyle.

The distinction between contemporary worship and the early church is the visceral understanding of worship of the early Christians. The Pharisees concerned themselves with outward acts of piety. The Early church concerned itself with centering on a communal worship of God.

WHAT WORSHIP IS

Lifestyle Worship may seem to be a foreign concept to many. The attitude for many Christians is, let's *go to* Worship, as if it is an event to plan, participate, and leave. Harold Best offers his definition of Worship:

> Worship is continuing in His presence while we continue to grow up into the stature of the fullness of Christ. Thus, we do not go to church to worship, nor are any activities meant to lead us into that state, for that state has already been brought about by redemption. Instead, we go to church, already at worship, but now to continue our worship corporately. This kind of worship is by faith alone unto more faith alone. We do

> not sing in order to worship; we sing because we worship.
>
> Continuous worship being our only possible state, our entire lives then become living epistles in which everything that we do, day in, day out, moment by moment, is marked by being a living sacrifice, worshipping in the continuum of spirit and truth and marking our sojourn of the beauty of holiness . . ."[11]

Some of our postmodern churches take a Humanistic-Christian attitude towards "fixing worship" problems. Instead of Faith, they rely on "best procedures" or "continuity of flow," or whatever seems right at the time. The early church concerned itself with centering on communal and holistic acts of worshipping God. They relied on faith.

Lifestyle Worship is the mind, spirit, and body coming into sync with God by faith. To limit worship to an event is enslaving Christianity to a building and rarely taking the Good News (Gospel) to the world. When we freely worship, as we should, we are demonstrating the power and beauty of God to everyone. Lifestyle worship is the result of our intimate interaction with God.

---

11. Best, Harold. "Worship, Faith, Grace, and Music Making Event: Worship! LA (Christian Worship Conference)," para 11–15.

Part Two

Lifestyle Worship

4

The A.D.D. Saint

I LEFT the house around nine in the morning on the first day of Christmas vacation. My three brothers and two sisters were either sleeping or watching television. I was determined to create some excitement by trekking out into the two hundred acres my parents owned in northwest Michigan. I followed a well-trodden trail and weaved through a grove of pine trees before I came upon my favorite hill. It was the top of a ridge that opened up into vast area of sand now covered in a thick blanket of snow; a perfect place to fly down the side of a steep hill.

The wind whistled as it grabbed the top layer of snow and violently threw it into the air causing it to fly into powdery dust and disappear. Again and again it whirled and whistled, biting into my cheeks. I pulled my scarf higher onto my nose and pulled my sled another foot up the steep incline to the top of my favorite sledding hill. I was beginning to question my sanity for staying out in this frigid weather. I was ten.

After sledding for about half an hour I decided that this would be my final run down the hill. I stepped back, threw the sled down, and jumped on it only to hit a bump just seconds after getting on. I tumbled off and slid half way down the hill. When I finally came to a stop, I rolled over and smacked my hand in anger into the frozen snow. As I did, I heard the snow crack under the force of my hand. I gathered my sled and started the long, cold walk back home.

As I trudged through the snow, I fought the bitter wind by leaning forward with my head down. I listened to the wind as it howled around me. I heard the snow crunch and give way beneath my boots as I labored to make my way home. Just as I reached the trail that would lead me to the house, the wind abruptly stopped blowing. I stopped, stood up straight, turned, and looked behind me. I listened, but heard nothing.

I didn't know at the time what a terrific impact this would have on me. All I could hear was my heavy breathing. I tried to control it to catch a sound of something. Nothing. Complete silence. Raised in a large family, it was odd to be surrounded by silence. I was too young to completely process this wonderful moment. All I remember thinking was, "It's nice to be in the quiet."

THE BLINK OF THINK

Lifestyle Worship begins with our *proskunetes* act of worship, which requires time alone with God. We are surrounded by voices that try to influence us to buy, sell, behave, feel, and do. There is a distinct connection between the voices and noise we hear and the inability to connect with God. We live in an energized culture that moves at the blink of think. Adrenaline rush is the drug of choice. The busier we become the happier we think we are. Without conditioning our lives to live at a rested pace, we will eventually be stopped. It may happen in the form of a failed relationship, a death, legal action, or some other collision course. Hundreds of books are written on the topic of time management and slowing down. It is not enough to slow down, we must stop and allow ourselves time for God. We can either react to our pace of life or choose to live within God's schedule.

Webster defines quiet as: (1) Characterized by an absence or near absence of agitation or activity; (2) Free of noise or uproar; or making little if any sound; (3) Free from disturbance.[1] The majority of Hebrew and Greek words for quiet or peace all have the same common connotation: to be in a restful state. For example, the Hebrew word Shaqat (shaw-kat) has the meaning of being undisturbed, tranquil, and quiet, as found in Isaiah 30:15, "In repentance and rest is your salvation, in quietness and trust is your strength, but you would have none of it." Isn't it interesting that quiet is associated with strength? If we don't find solitude, rest, peace, or tranquility in our life, how are we to strengthen our relationship with God? Listen to Job as he cries out, "I have no peace, no quietness; I have no rest, but only turmoil," (Job 3:2). Here, Job uses the same word Shaqat (shä-kat') to express his frustration. Many of us get frustrated like Job because we cry out to God to help us and nothing happens. When we are not at peace with ourselves we have no quietness. We are not surrendering our activity to God.

The Greek counterpart to Shaqat is Hesuchios (hay-soo'-khee-os), which also means quiet or tranquil as illustrated in I Peter, ". . . it should be that of your inner self, the unfading beauty of a gentle and *quiet* spirit, which is of

1. Merriam–Webster Online Dictionary, 2008, s.v. "Quiet."

great worth in God's sight,"(1 Peter 3:4—emphasis added). How we see our walk with God is not necessarily the way he sees it. What is it that God loves to look at? A quiet spirit. If we want God to act, we must be willing to be still and quiet, taking time to know him.

BE STILL AND KNOW

To arrive at a place of quiet in our hearts means to physically be at rest. Psalms 46:10 makes it clear that we are to, "Be *still*, and *know* that I am God . . ." The Hebrew word *still* is *Raphah* (*raw-faw*), which means: *to be quiet, to relax, withdraw, to let drop, abandon, relax, to let go*. This verse has two separate statements that have one meaning: Be *still* and *know*. The Hebrew word for *know* is *Yada* (*yaw-dah*), which translates: *to know, to perceive, to find out and discern, to know by experience*. How can we know God by experience if we are not still or quiet? It is a choice we must make if we truly long to develop a relationship with God.

Children have a difficult time standing still. The curiosity of life around them is too enticing to stop and be quiet. When it involves spending time alone with God adults are not much different. We become enamored with life around us instead of learning to know the One inside us.

My friend Kim Hutchcroft plays the saxophone. He doesn't just play for pleasure; he plays for a living as a studio musician. He is one of the founding members of the Grammy nominated 70s jazz band *Seawind* and is now one of the most sought after studio musicians in the world. He has played on albums too numerous to mention, six hit movie soundtracks, and has appeared with or played on albums with BB King, Michael Jackson, Frank Sinatra, Quincy Jones, Kenny G, Dolly Parton, Michael McDonald, Diana Ross, George Benson, Christopher Cross, and the list goes on.

Like any master musician, Kim didn't make it to the top of the music industry by practicing the saxophone occasionally. He studied and practiced daily until he reached a level of professional proficiency. He knows (*yada*) his instrument, and practice and experience has made him the best in the business. He still practices daily to continually fine-tune his craft.

Practicing lifestyle worship requires an act of discipleship, the disciplining of our spiritual lives. Brother Lawrence uses the term, *holy habits* to help us understand the development of discipline. Becoming quiet takes energy. It requires a restructuring of our life to create *holy habits.*

It is easier to sit in front of the television and have someone entertain us than to take the energy to quiet our minds and come into God's glorious presence. Why is it that we are able to have a consistent timetable with regards to television yet we are unable to interact with God, who longs to have an intimate relationship with us? God desires an equitable relationship, one where we interact, speak, listen, and understand. It is difficult to love the Light of the world when we are distracted by the light of our TV. We find in 1 Thessalonians 4:11 that we are to, ". . . study to be *quiet*, and to do your own business, and to work with your own hands . . ." (KJV, emphasis added). The New American Standard Bible translates this verse: ". . . and to make it your ambition to lead a *quiet* life and attend to your own business and work with your hands . . ." (emphasis added).

Early in my ministry I was very ambitious. But to be honest, it was not to be quiet and discipline my life. My goals and aspirations were more self-centered than to think about being quiet. I had a family and many responsibilities. Frankly, this verse was just one of many that blurred in and out of my spiritual vision. It was one of those verses that was for someone else. I felt I must maintain a certain spiritual composure for my flock, when in reality, I desperately needed to find quiet in my life. To recondition our thought process we must first stop and consider what our true desires are. The more we desire to spend time being entertained by the vices and cunning characters portrayed in movies and television, the less we desire to be with God.

The act of being still and knowing comes from a lifestyle of discipline. Dallas Willard remarks, "A baseball player who expects to excel in the game without adequate exercise of his body is no more ridiculous than the Christian who hopes to be able to act in the manner of Christ when put to the test without appropriate exercise in godly living."[2]

Our rushing around and need for activity reflects our true spiritual condition. Attentiveness to the inward voice is the mitigating factor that enables us to either seek out activity forcing our internal turmoil to be capped like a pressure cooker or allow us to long for the quiet to hear God's voice and release our innermost concerns. There were days I did not want to make the time to listen. Listening takes energy. Coming home after committee meetings or counseling sessions drained me. It took all I had to find the energy to be attentive to my family. However, I began to pray that

2. Willard, Dallas, *The Spirit of Disciplines: understanding how God changes lives*, 4–5.

God would give me the desire and energy to listen. Slowly, I took a few minutes before I went to bed and spent time alone with God. I practiced spending less time in front of my computer and TV and forced myself to go into another room or outdoors to pray.

An athlete must go through exercise and conditioning before he or she competes. For me, the conditioning and exercising was just being still. I forced myself to calm my thoughts and learn to be quiet. It was difficult because I wanted to think about work, finances, or my family. It may seem silly to equate sitting with exercise, and calming your mind as conditioning, but it really does take energy to be still. Some people think it is like being in Drive all day long and suddenly throwing your life into Park. Instead, it should be a time to slowly calm your body and mind after a hectic day, a time to relax and enjoy the quiet. In the beginning, it may seem like a difficult task because we have been conditioned to go. David Kundtz says, "Stopping is doing nothing as much as possible, for a definite period of time . . . for the purpose of becoming more fully awake and remembering who you are . . . The ultimate reason for stopping is going."[3]

Whether we know it or not, we are often meditating. How many times have you watched a television program or a movie and thought about it for the next day or so, or discussed it with others? What you are doing is meditating about the subject matter of the event. It takes little physical effort to be entertained. However, it takes energy to stay awake and pray or meditate.

3. Kundtz, "Stopping: How to Be Still When You Have to Keep Going," para 5.

Why is it that we believe what the Bible says is true, yet ignore the difficult sayings and skip to the warm fuzzies? What many Christians fail to realize is the amazing and incredible experience they could have if they would only stop, wait, and listen. I equate it to lifting weights: it hurts, it sometimes aches, and it takes discipline to exercise everyday, but soon you see the results. The muscle must tear down in order to build up stronger. It is in the same manner that we must tear down our fleshly desires and spend time with God to become stronger.

CHURCH-ATIZED

When do we have time to listen to God? We race from work, to home, to our TV or computer. Some of us are being "Church-atized" by spending much of our time attending a multitude of church functions, thinking that we are learning more *about* God instead of getting to *know* God.

Critics may ask, "Is this a bad thing?" The problem arises when there is no balance between our contemplative time with God and our fellowship time with other believers. We need the interaction and knowledge from our spiritual leaders and friends. But, we also need our quiet times with God. The Act of Quiet is an integral part of disciplining our spiritual life.

Thich Nhat Hanh, a Vietnamese born Buddhist, rallied his countrymen during the Vietnam War to aid in rebuilding villages. He was also an outspoken crusader for peace. Because of his activist ways (although peaceful) he was exiled from Vietnam. His actions and writings soon garnered the praise and friendships of Martin Luther King and Thomas Merton. In 1967 King nominated Hanh for the Nobel Peace prize. With ecumenical insight, Hanh writes, "Discussing God is not the best use of our energy, we touch God not as a concept but as a living reality."[4]

Many Christians who believe in God in theory are Humanistic-Christians or those that rely on their own power to care for their lives rather than allow Faith to be predominant in every activity of life. Lifestyle Worship requires us to come to a place of rest. Not simply slowing down to catch the next sermon at church and move on to the next activity, but to stop and wait. Stopping is not a desirable option in our blink and think culture but it is a necessity if we truly want to know God.

THE DISCIPLINE OF QUIET

Tom Brown Jr. is recognized as the most renowned Tracker, Wilderness, and Survival expert in North America. His skills have assisted police in solving numerous homicide cases and finding forty missing persons. Tom didn't become a gifted Tracker overnight. He has studied Nature and its nuances for many years.

In his book *The Tracker* he takes us through his childhood years growing up, along with his best friend Rich, under the tutelage of an old Apache Indian called Stalking Wolf. Tom and Rich spent every free moment learning how to survive and become a part of nature. The lessons learned reach deeper than those of just tracking. Much of what Stalking Wolf taught the boys was to be still and observe.

---

4. Hanh, *Living Buddha, Living Christ*, 21.

One day Stalking Wolf asked the boys to feed the birds. A general request that the boys knew was not as simple as it sounded since Stalking Wolf had no pet birds. They were aware that he had a deeper lesson in store for them than simply feeding the birds of the air. After pondering it for a day, they asked Stalking Wolf how they should feed the birds. Stalking Wolf replied, "How would you feed me?" Tom answered, "I would hand you the food." Stalking Wolf smiled and turned away.

They knew exactly what he meant and the next morning they woke up early and headed to the woods. They found a clearing and laid on their backs with arms outstretched, birdseed in hand. They waited. They were quiet. And they waited some more. The art of birds eating from your hand is the art of being still (quiet). Tom and Rich practiced being still and became masters at it. In the beginning it was uncomfortable. It was hard to lie on the ground with arms outstretched. It was difficult to learn how to breathe properly. It wasn't easy to control thoughts and urges. But soon, it became natural and birds began to confidently swoop down and perch on their fingers to peck the birdseed from their hands. Once Tom and Rich stepped out of their comfort zone, they were able to experience a more rewarding and abundant life. A repeated practice of stillness gave them a joy that very few are privileged to enjoy.

God wants to bless us abundantly. God desires to develop a relationship with us as found in Revelation 3:20, "Here I am! I stand at the door and knock. If you hear my voice and open the door, I will come in and eat with you, and you will eat with me," (New Century Version). God wants to bless us and feed us, but we first must be willing to listen to hear his voice speaking to us.

The art of listening and waiting have become lost in the busyness of our culture. In his timely book, CrazyBusy, Dr. Edward Hallowell says that, ". . . lingering is a lost art. Such is our hurry and our need for constant stimulation that a modern romantic conversation might go like this: "I love you." "Oh good, now what's your next point?". . . if we're not careful, we'll get so busy that we will miss taking the time to think and feel."[5]

The problem is that we don't know how to be still. Many decisions have been in haste because it is easier to react than it is to wait. We have become so absorbed in the frenzied world around us that we have lost sight of God's yearning for intimacy with us. Without alone time with him we will never experience that peace that transcends all understanding (Philippians 4:7).

ALONE

The practice of lifestyle worship involves a significant act of physical and mental discipline. How many times have you heard someone talk in terms of "being busy" or having a "busy day"? While teaching a college course on Personal Development, I asked my students what the first thing they did after they got into their car and started it. The overwhelming response was: "Turn the radio on!" Almost every student complained that they couldn't stand being alone. They thrived on noise. For a class project, I had them spend

---

5. Hallowell, *Crazybusy: Overstretched, Overbooked, and about to snap!*, 20.

two hours alone and write a paper about their experience. The outcome was what I expected. It wasn't a problem finding the time but it was a mental challenge to deal with their inner self. Most of the students struggled with facing their own thoughts.

Many Christians are no different; they don't like to approach solitude. Being alone with your thoughts means issues in your life must be dealt with. Attitudes may need to be adjusted, which requires letting go of cancerous anger or a controlling behavior that has become a comfortable but evil friend.

There is no escaping the reality that we live in a noise-filled world. How we cope with noise and distractions is the choice we must make. When coming home from a harried day, it may help to let your spouse and children know that you need ten minutes or half an hour to be alone. Susanna Wesley, the mother of evangelists Charles and John Wesley, had a unique way of finding time alone with God in the busyness of life. Living in a home with more than ten children she would sit down at the dinner table and pull her apron up over her head. She would use this time to pray. Her children knew this was her alone time and not to disturb her. Some units of the British Army wear their hats to breakfast to let others know they do not want to be disturbed. The author of Lamentations 3:25–28 has this to say about being silent before God, "The LORD is good to those whose hope is in him, to the one who seeks him; it is good to wait quietly for the salvation of the LORD. It is good for a man to bear the yoke while he is young. Let him sit alone in silence, for the LORD has laid it on him," (emphasis added).

It is good to wait for God. In order to seek God we must wait quietly. This command comes with a blessing: if we hope, seek, and wait quietly, the Lord is good to us. Why is it that we are quick to do our 15 minute devotionals, offer our service on a church committee, sing in the choir, or teach a Sunday School class, yet we can't sit alone in silence?

Most writers on the thoughts of quiet, solitude and the steps to a deeper relationship with God make the distinct statement that we must discipline our lives to know God better:

- Brother Lawrence challenges us to, ". . . Hold yourself in prayer before God like a dumb or paralytic beggar at a rich man's gate."[6]

- Thomas á Kempis cries out that we must, ". . . lay the axe to the root [of sin]. . ."[7]

- Thomas Merton warns, "Keep your eyes clean and your ears quiet and your mind serene."[8]

- Teresa of Avila counsels, "I consider it quite certain that those who attain perfection do not ask the Lord to deliver them from trials, temptations, persecutions, and conflicts . . ."[9]

A simple act such as denying yourself TV time in exchange for prayer is an act of discipline. Fasting is simply denying ourselves of worldly pleasures for the benefit of

6. Lawrence, Brother. *The Practice of The Presence of God*, 8th Letter.

7. á Kempis, Thomas. *Devotional Classics*, 186.

8. Merton, Thomas. *New Seeds of Contemplation*, 86.

9. Teresa, Avila. *The Way of Perfection*, chapter 38.

spiritual gain. How do we expect to live forever with God and rest in the luxury of his amazing love and presence without getting to know him now?

GOD'S VOICE

When Jesus took Peter, James, and John to a high mountain, he became transfigured and his face was as bright as the sun. Suddenly, Moses and Elijah appeared and were talking with Jesus. What Jesus, Moses, and Elijah were talking about isn't recorded. What is recorded is the voice of God coming from a cloud that encompasses the party on the mountain. He speaks, "This is my Son, whom I love; with him I am well pleased. *Listen to him!* (Matthew 17:5—emphasis added).

The Bible is our standard, our handbook for living a victorious Christian life, but it not to be a substitute for listening to God's voice. The word of God *is* God's word. We find in Roman's 10:17, "... faith comes by hearing, and hearing by the *word* of God," (NKJV—emphasis added). The word for *word* is the Greek word *rhema* (hray'-mah), which means: *that which is or has been uttered by the living voice, thing spoken, any sound produced by the voice and having definite meaning.* I once heard a pastor errantly quote this scripture and say that since he was reading God's word (the Bible) we will now grow in faith. The Bible is called God's *word* and without a doubt it is. However, Paul conveys the meaning of listening to God's present voice. This Greek word *rhema* is also found in the following verses (emphasis added):

- "It is written, 'Man shall not live by bread alone, but by every *word* that proceeds from the mouth of God," (Matthew 4:4—NKJV). The New Century Version translates this verse, stating that Jesus answered, "It is written in the Scriptures, 'A person does not live by eating only bread, but by everything God says.'"
- "Take the helmet of salvation, and the sword of the Spirit, which is the *word* of God," (Ephesians 6:17—NIV).
- ". . . but the *word* of the Lord stands forever," (1 Peter 1:25—NIV).

These are just a few verses that illustrate God's voice speaking out. If God desires to speak to us, why aren't we listening? What is hindering you from hearing God?

LISTENING

Sounds are distractions. Distractions seem to feed on many Christians' opportunities for quiet. Instead of dwelling in solitude, they would rather dwell in noise. Listening means we cease talking. Kahlil Gibran says, "You talk when you cease to be at peace with your thoughts . . . And when you can no longer dwell in the solitude of your heart you live in your lips, and sound is a diversion and a pastime . . . There are those among you who seek the talkative through fear of being alone."[10]

If Gibran were alive today he might revise his thoughts and say, "There are those among you who seek the internet,

10. Gibran, Kahlil. *The Prophet*, chapter 20.

music, chatter, gossip, and other noise, for fear of being alone." To listen means we must focus our thoughts on the One we are listening to.

To listen takes energy. The lack of listening causes laziness in our spirit, which in turn quenches our ability to hear from God. Even in the distractions of a busy monastery kitchen Brother Lawrence found solitude in his heart, "For me the time of action does not differ from the time of prayer, and in the noise and clatter of my kitchen, while several persons are together calling for as many different things, I possess God in as great tranquility as when upon my knees..."[11]

Brother Lawrence didn't arrive at the Carmelite Monastery with an endowed understanding of the mind of God. As a matter-of-fact, when he first came to the Monastery, he despised working in the kitchen. For many years he labored at a job he disliked. He soon discovered that a change in attitude could result in a life-altering experience. He decided to rejoice at the opportunity to clean discarded food off plates, and scour baked on grease off pots and pans. Later in life, Brother Lawrence continued to experience God as he mended shoes for his Brothers at the Monastery. He was a revered monk who found joy and contentment in the simple things of life. It was simply a change in attitude.

In his classic book, *The Celebration of Disciplines*, Richard Foster notes, "Superficiality is the curse of our age. The doctrine of instant satisfaction is a primary spiritual problem. The desperate need today is not for a greater number of intelligent people, or gifted people, but for deep

11. Lawrence, *Brother*, 12.

people."[12] When we think of deep people do we think of saints of old, or monks who committed themselves to monastic prayers all day long? In reality we are all called to a deeper walk with God, ". . . but God has revealed it to us by his Spirit. The Spirit searches all things, even the deep things of God," (1 Corinthians 2:10). We are called to a relationship with God. We sometimes associate deep thinkers or deep people with Saints or Mystics.

SAINTS & MYSTICS

As Christians we believe in a spiritual world. But how often do we allow the spiritual world and the physical world to meet? I like John Ortberg's explanation of bringing the spiritual world into our natural world. He says, ". . . make up there come down here." Based on Jesus' prayer (commonly referred to as The Lord's Prayer), ". . . your kingdom come, your will be done on earth as it is in Heaven." Ortberg says, "This is maybe the most dangerous, exciting, life-altering prayer a human being can pray: 'God, make up there come down here'. . . Start by asking yourself this question: 'Where do I want God's presence and power to break into my world? Where would I especially like God to use me to make things down here run the way they do up there?'"[13]

We often refer to saints or mystics as people with unusual perseverance when it comes to interacting with the

12. Foster, Richard. *Celebration of Discipline: The Path to Spiritual Growth*, 1.

13. Ortberg, *God Is Closer Than You Think: This Can Be the Greatest Moment of Your Life Because This Moment Is the Place Where You Can Meet God*, 161.

spiritual world. The word Saint or Saints appears in the Bible over 90 times. In the New Testament the word hagios (hag'-ee-os) is the same word used for Saint and for Holy, as in the Holy Ghost. The word Mystic or Mysticism does not occur in the Bible at all. It wasn't until the mid Fourteenth Century that it was used. Today, we call great men and women of God who lived their lives in a holy manner mystics. Brother Lawrence, Julian of Norwich, George Fox, Theresa of Avila, Madame Guyon, St. John of The Cross, and A.W. Tozer are a few of the men and women associated with Christian mysticism.

For many modern Christians the word mysticism may conjure up visions of Tibetan monks sitting cross-legged on the edge of a mountain chanting, "Omm, Omm, Omm." We automatically attribute mysticism to Eastern religions such as Buddhism, Hinduism, Sufism, and the like. However, the true meaning of mysticism or a mystic is one who aspires to connect with God, and was first used in reference to men and women who had a deeper understanding of God than those of their day.

The Merriam-Webster Dictionary defines mysticism as: "the belief that direct knowledge of God, spiritual truth, or ultimate reality can be attained through subjective experience (as intuition or insight)."[14] The Cambridge Dictionary interprets it more directly: "the belief that there is hidden meaning in life or that each human being can unite with God."[15] And the Compact Oxford English Dictionary defines a mystic as: "a person who seeks by contemplation and self-surrender to attain unity with the Deity and reach

14. Merriam-Webster Online Dictionary, 2008, s.v. "Mysticism."
15. Cambridge University Press, 2008, s.v. "Mysticism."

truths beyond human understanding."[16] Jon Zuck explains Christian mysticism this way:

> To know God directly shows that mysticism is different from any passive or legalistic kind of Christianity. It means:
>
> - That while we honor the Scripture, we want to know God directly, not just through Scripture.
> - While we respect our heritage of teachings about God, we want to know God directly, not through doctrines and teachings.
> - While we gather in communal worship, we want to know God directly, not just through the Church.[17]

A mystic is simply a Christian that connects with God, someone who walks in continual worship. The reason Brother Lawrence, Madame Guyon, St. John of the Cross, and others were labeled mystics was that they made the *up there come down here*. It is not a spiritual mystery to be labeled a mystic. It is only a word. However, the action behind what this word defines is the difference between one who connects with God (knows him), and one who does not have a relationship and believes in him in theory (Humanistic-Christian).

We are either a Christian Mystic or a Humanistic-Christian. We are either aspiring to know God (Matt. 7:21–23) or we are not. How can we say that we are children

---

16. Compact Oxford English Dictionary. 2008, s.v. "Mysticism."
17. Zuck, John. "What is Christian Mysticism?," para. 6

of God (John 1:12) if we aren't getting to know our Father? How can we declare that Jesus lives within us (Galatians 2:20) if we only believe it in theory?

The Saints of scripture and the Christian Mystics of old were one in the same. The early believers didn't need another word for who they were and how they were to live. They understood without question. They knew that in order to know God they must bring the spiritual world into the natural world, the *up there, down here.*

5

Know God

ONE OF my favorite stories is about two men on a platform in a crowded auditorium with standing room only. The first, a handsome, well-dressed young man, rose from his seat and walked briskly to the podium. "The Lord is my Shepherd . . ." he began with the eloquence of a great orator, ". . . I shall not want . . ." When he finished the Twenty-third Psalm the crowd leaped to their feet and began cheering and clapping. Never before had they heard such a beautiful prayer.

After a few minutes of applause and kudos to the young man, the crowd settled down. The second, an old man who was commonly dressed, pulled himself up with his cane and hobbled to the podium. "The Lord . . . is my Shepherd . . ." he began, his voice rough and sometimes crackling. When he finished, he turned and slowly made his way back to his seat. It was obvious he was not as skilled a speaker as the young man was. The crowd didn't cheer. They didn't applaud. But something strange began to happen. Some people were crying, some praying, some sitting stunned. After a few brief moments, the young man walked to the podium and said, "Ladies and gentleman. I would like to explain what has happened here. You see, I know the

Twenty-third Psalm. But my friend here . . . he knows the Shepherd."

How many of us truly know God? Would you get married and never try to get to know your spouse? It would be absurd to think a relationship would grow if all you ever did was listen to what other people had to say about your spouse. A positive relationship is one where communication is open, honest, and two-way. Many Christians think it is enough to believe in God. Do we quickly forget that even the demons "believe" (James 2:19)?

TASHA & JOHN

The courtship process for most industrialized cultures is intended to offer the exchange of personal information between a man and a woman. After analyzing the behavior and information gathered, the two individuals may decide to pursue a deeper relationship. Through active communication, they may discover they have found a suitable life partner, and if so, marriage is the inevitable outcome. However, this process is often short-circuited in many relationships because the two acquaintances decide to forego the *getting to know you* stage and jump to the *sexual stage* (the marriage stage without being married) of the relationship. In my counseling practice, I have worked with numerous couples that, after many years of marriage, struggle with their spouse because they skipped an integral part of their relationship.

Many Christians suffer the same consequences as those pursuing a dating relationship. When we become Christians many of us short-circuit our romance with God.

We won't wait and listen. It's easier to ignore the discipline and meat of Christianity and run to church to eat our dessert. Consider this scenario:

Tasha and John meet at a coffee shop and instantly have a strong attraction for each other. John never asks Tasha anything about her likes, dislikes, hobbies, dreams, or anything that would help him get to know her. Instead he consults her friends for information about her. But some of her friends have jaded views of Tasha and warn John to be careful. Like John, Tasha did not take the time to get to know John. Instead she enlists the help of his friends to tell her everything about John. Like Tasha's friends, some of John's friends were not truly friends.

For Christmas Tasha buys John a red sweater because one of John's friends told her he liked the color red. John's favorite color is blue and he hates sweaters and prefers cotton twill shirts. For her birthday, John buys Tasha a beautiful gold ring. A close friend of Tasha's told John she likes gold and loves rings. Tasha dislikes gold rings but loves silver necklaces.

Our relationship with God is eerily similar to Tasha and John's relationship. It seems it is easier for us to listen to other people tell us about God and what he is like rather than find out for ourselves. What others tell us about God may not always be the truth. So why don't we find out for ourselves?

FLEETING MOMENTS OF AFFECTION

I recently read Jane Dobisz's candid book, *The Wisdom of Solitude: A Zen Retreat In The Woods*. She is one of the few women fully authorized as a Buddhist Zen Master. Dobisz shares how she retreats to a secluded cabin for a few weeks to find release from her frustration and anxieties through daily rituals of disciplined meditation. As I 'meditated' on her retreat in the woods I soon realized that she did experience some positives from her retreat. She eagerly disciplined herself to increase her bowing time, she fought to control her desire for food and other fleshly cravings, and she had a heightened awareness of ordinary chores. Although she experienced emotional and physical cleansing, she didn't have a connection to anything except herself and her surroundings.

In stark contrast to Dobisz, my friend, Author/ Songwriter/ Grammy-nominated/ Dove Award winner Margaret Becker, shared her retreat experience in *Coming Up For Air*. Here we find Margaret seeking to find peace in her life by retreating to a house on a quiet beach in Florida. We follow her struggles to come to terms with herself and her relationship with her heavenly Father. Margaret and Jane both struggle in the same way to find peace in the chaos of their lives. However, the striking difference is that, although Jane was able to lower her blood pressure and become more disciplined, she didn't relate to anything except herself.

Many Humanistic-Christians have the same experience when they leave a church service. They feel good. There is nothing wrong with how we feel after a church service. But, if we did not connect with God, that is, truly experience him and not just a euphoric feeling, then we are no different than Buddhists, Muslims, or Hindus. Again, Brother Lawrence, "It is not enough to know God as theory, from what we read in books, or feel some fleeting moments of affection for him, brief as the wave of feeling, or glimpse of the Divine . . . our faith must be alive, and we must make it so, and by means lift ourselves beyond all these passing emotions to worship the Father and Jesus Christ in all their divine perfection. This path of faith is the spirit of the Church and will lead to great perfection,"[1] (emphasis added).

Margaret found a connection on her retreat. She struggled, she hurt, and she was uncomfortable. But she stood steadfast, sometimes in silence. She moved beyond the *fleeting motions of affection* and discovered a deep, rich, life-changing relationship with God. She took the time to know her Shepherd.

KNOW ME

If someone were to ask you what God has been directly speaking to you about, what would you answer? Could you answer? Hebrews 3:15 declares, ". . . Today, if you hear his voice, do not harden your hearts . . ." We find in Isaiah 28:23 that God is very direct in his command for us to be attentive, "Listen and hear my voice; pay attention and hear what I say." We can only hear when we stop to listen and become quiet and worship.

One of the reasons God calls us to quietness, to still our lives even during terrible disturbances, is to help us to know him. Many people will be sadly disappointed when they stand before God. Jesus makes this very clear in Matthew 7: 21–23, "Not everyone who says to me, 'Lord, Lord,' will enter the kingdom of Heaven, but only he who does the will of my Father who is in Heaven. Many will say to me on that

1. Lawrence.

day, 'Lord, Lord, did we not prophesy in your name, and in your name drive out demons and perform many miracles?' Then will I tell them plainly, 'I never knew (yada) you. Away from me you evildoers!'" (parenthesis added).

God wants us to know him by experiencing his miraculous ways. He wants to have a relationship with us, but many are unwilling to spend time getting to know him. It is very interesting that immediately after he makes this stirring statement in Matthew 7:21–23 he immediately follows with, "Therefore everyone who hears these *words* (rhema) of mine and puts them into practice . . ." (emphasis added) and proceeds to tell the story of the wise man building his house on a firm foundation, and the foolish man who build his house on the sand, "Therefore everyone who hears these words of mine and puts them into practice is like a wise man who built his house on the rock. The rain came down, the streams rose, and the winds blew and beat against that house; yet it did not fall, because it had its foundation on the rock. But everyone who hears these words of mine and does not put them into practice is like a foolish man who built his house on sand. The rain came down, the streams rose, and the winds blew and beat against that house, and it fell with a great crash," (Matthew 7:24–27).

Luke 6:46–49 adds more emphasis, "Why do you call me, 'Lord, Lord,' and do not do what I say? I will show you what he is like who comes to me and hears my words and puts them into practice. He is like a man building a house, who dug down deep and laid the foundation on rock. When a flood came, the torrent struck that house but could not shake it, because it was well built. But the one who hears my words and does not put them into practice is like a man who built a house on the ground without a foundation. The moment the torrent struck that house, it collapsed and its destruction was complete."

Our foundation is built on how strong our relationship with God is. Sadly, many of us won't spend time alone with God. We are unknowingly building our foundation on sand. I find it interesting that Jesus didn't say the wise man built his house on solid ground. The word he uses is petra, which literally means a rock or rocky ground. He could have used the word ge (ghay) for ground, as found in the following verses (emphasis added):

- "But he that received seed into the good *ground* is he that heareth the word, and understandeth [it]; which also beareth fruit, and bringeth forth, some an hundredfold, some sixty, some thirty." (Matthew 13:23—KJV)

- "Verily, verily, I say unto you, except a corn of wheat fall into the *ground* and die, it abideth alone: but if it die, it bringeth forth much fruit." (John 12:24—KJV)

- "Then said the Lord to him, 'Put off thy shoes from thy feet: for the place where thou standest is holy *ground*.'" (Acts 7:33—KJV)

Doesn't that seem odd? Why would he use the word petra which means rock instead of the word ground? A rock is a rough and very hard object. You would need to drill down deep into the rock to get a strong, solid hold on the foundation. Building a house on rock takes more time to build than a house built on sand, but it will not move.

The Christian whose strong house was built on rock is the one who spends time with the Chief Contractor and is given instruction on how to complete the project. He speaks to us. God speaks to us, if we are quiet and take the time to listen. There are almost one hundred instances of God's voice speaking to man throughout scripture. If God didn't want to speak to us, we would all be puppets on a string with no will or desire for God. But to hear God's voice we need to be quiet.

What is also interesting about this passage of scripture is the word he uses for *foolish*. He could have used the word *aphfron (af'-ron)*, which means *foolish, stupid, or acting rashly*. Instead, Jesus uses the word *moros (mo-ros)*, which has the meaning of being *godless*. He is describing two types of people: those that know him and those that say they know him in theory.

As Christians, we don't want to say that we are *godless*. That's absurd. However, many of us have a godless relationship. In theory, we believe in God. In reality, we are too busy to develop an intimate relationship with him. Kierkegaard utters these strong words of caution, "The apostasy from Christianity will not come about openly by everybody renouncing Christianity; no, but slyly, cunningly, knavishly, by everybody assuming the name of being Christian, thinking that in this way all were most securely secured against . . . Christianity, the Christianity of the New Testament, which people are afraid of, and therefore industrial priests have invented under the name of Christianity a sweetmeat which has a delicious taste, for which men hand out money with delight."[2]

2. Lowrie, *Kierkegaard's Attack Upon Christendom*, 46–47.

If we look at this entire section and put it into perspective, what do we see? First, Jesus says if we don't know him we will never be able to be in his presence. Second, he tells us that if we hear his words and put them into practice we will be like the wise man. If we use wisdom and discipline (practice) ourselves to spiritual training we will be just like the wise man who took his time (quieted his life and listened to God), labored hard (disciplined his life by getting before God instead of his TV), and was able to resist the storm (temptation). He therefore lived a wonderful, Jesus-centered life because he took the time to know God.

If we don't take time to know him, we are like the foolish man, the god-less man, the one who really doesn't have a relationship with God. I don't want to be like the foolish man who isn't able to be in God's presence because he didn't take the time to develop a relationship with his heavenly Father. Best selling author Ted Dekker puts it this way, ". . . if your passion for being with Christ isn't greater by far than remaining in this life (as Paul characterized his desire for heaven), then your motive for following Christ is suspicious (according to Christ)."[3]

Energy. It takes time, energy, and passion to cultivate love and desire to be with God. Relationships don't happen overnight. Jesus uses this parable to wake us up. I was too busy with ministry to spend time developing a relationship with God. I had a flock to develop relationships with. I was the foolish man. Godless. I was living a Humanistic-Christian life, a life without a relationship with God.

---

3. Dekker, *The Slumber of Christianity: Awakening A Passion for Heaven on Earth*, 106.

THE THREE LITTLE PIGS

Another wonderful analogy of these verses in Matthew is the story of the Three Little Pigs. The first pig builds his house out of straw. He truly believed it was strong enough to keep out the big, bad wolf. Sadly, he was mistaken. The second pig was a tad smarter and built his house out of sticks; a little stronger than straw, but not strong enough to keep the wolf out. The third little pig decided to take his time and do it right. He wasn't anxious or worried. He built his house out of bricks and of course it withstood the mighty wind of the wily wolf.

I needed to pause in my life to determine how I was building my relationship with God. Like the first pig, I was building my relationship out of straw, by thinking that going to church was enough or by socializing with other Christians and giving them the impression that I had it all together. I realized I needed to take God a little more seriously, but I found myself in a holding pattern. Like the second little pig, I used my sticks by taking a little bit more time and throwing up prayers to God. But it was one-sided. I would talk, but didn't give God the time of day. I religiously did my devotions every day, but didn't devote my whole being to God. I gave him the ten or twenty minutes a day I thought he deserved. Yes, it was more than building a relationship out of straw, but I wasn't spending time getting to know a relational God. For a period of time I was content with my life. I could call myself a Christian and even work full time in the ministry, but I wasn't satisfied.

When I came across this passage in Matthew 7, I began to study it closer. I realized that God created us and he longs to speak to us, to have a relationship with us. How profound, yet how simple it is to understand that God desires two-way communication. My pilgrimage now is to drill down deep into the rock by disciplining myself to be quiet. I am now trying to take the time and build my house out of bricks . . . on a rock.

I read a story of a Police Officer stopping a woman driver. When the Officer asked the woman for her license and registration, the woman protested and asked why she was stopped. She informed the Officer that she wasn't speeding. The Officer nodded in agreement and said,

"No, I'm not stopping you for speeding."

"Then why did you stop me?" asked the woman.

"I saw a car swerve in front of you," began the Officer. "Then I saw you yell and scream at the other car. Am I correct so far?"

"Well, yes, that is correct," the woman said somewhat embarrassed. "But why did you stop me?"

The Officer paused and tipped his hat back, "Well, I saw the bumper stickers on the back of your car that say: *God is My Co-Pilot*, and *Life is short Pray hard,* and *WWJD,* and well, I thought the car was stolen."

Many of us are like the woman driver. On the outside we want everyone to know that we are right with God. But when we are faced with a defining situation, our Humanistic character rises to the occasion instead of God's love pouring through us.

God desires us and want us to have an intimate relationship with him. Richard Foster uses the term *God intoxicating experiences.*[4] But sometimes it's scary to step

4. Foster, *Prayer*, 71.

out in faith. Instead we take the safe route and take on a Humanistic-Christian mindset. We believe that although God exists, personal disturbances will be handled personally, void of faith in his miraculous ways. Because of this, we miss incredible *God intoxicating experiences.* Therefore our attitude is that faith is a large obstacle that is reserved for people who have time to be quiet and pray. But we always have a choice. God is waiting for us to wait, to stop and to be quiet.

ALONE WITH GOD

Great Christians of the past spent much of their time in contemplation. Contemplation is *(the) concentration on spiritual things as a form of private devotion; a state of mystical awareness of God's being; an act of considering with attention.*[5] The key to contemplation is being quiet. Listening. Waiting. Being available. God is longing to reach out and speak to us. The word contemplation is often used in the same context of prayer or meditation. However, contemplation also means to *separate something from its environment.* So, does this mean that during a hectic day or the rise of unexpected trials we have to search out and try to find a quiet place go through a mind-numbing time of meditation? Whether physically or spiritually separating ourselves, it is imperative to do as Jesus did and get away, either by locking yourself in the bathroom, going for a walk, putting your apron over your head, or just closing your eyes.

5. Merriam-Webster Online Dictionary, 2008, s.v. "Contemplation."

In the context of contemplation of God, it simply means to spiritually separate from the worldly environment. I recently saw a bumper sticker that said: MY CAR IS MY PRAYER CLOSET. We need to find time to seek God no matter where we are. If someone doesn't have the time for God, they are too busy and their priorities are not in order.

Indian peace activist Mahatma Gandhi was jailed on numerous occasions. He spent over 2000 days in jail, which translates to nearly six years. Most of which was in solitary confinement. Gandhi used his time in solitude to clear his mind, to contemplate, to meditate, and focus on the issues that mattered most in his life. The rest is history.

Lifestyle worship or contemplation is an act of obedience, an act of discipline. In the New Testament, we find Jesus and his disciples often getting away from the hustle and bustle to find quiet and devote more time to God in worship (Mark 6:30–31). Jesus understood the need to continually grow closer to his Father through quiet times together. Being alone in worship is a therapeutic, healing time with our Father. If Jesus did it, why aren't we doing it?

SOLITUDE AND PSYCHOLOGY

Solitude is no longer a closet topic. Psychologists are discovering that solitude is an effective healing tool. The late Dr. Ester Buchholz, former Director of the Steinhardt's School of Psychology Program at New York University, spent much of her career exploring the role of solitude as a curative aid for various disorders. Here are some tidbits of her thoughts on solitude and religion: "Meaningful alonetime, it turns out, is a powerful need and a necessary tonic in today's rapid-fire world. Indeed, solitude actually allows us to connect to others in a far richer way . . . Religion no longer provides a place for quiet retreat but instead offers 'megachurches' of social and secular amusement . . . Religion must provide time for prayer and meditation. And the relationship of the individual to God is one solution to the paradox of aloneness and relatedness. For religion to have its greatest appeal, it must allow time for solitude . . ."[6]

Psychology Today editor, Hara Estroff Marano echoes her sentiments:

> As the world spins faster and faster—or maybe it just seems that way when an email can travel around the world in fractions of a second—we mortals need a variety of ways to cope with the resulting pressures. We need to maintain some semblance of balance and some sense that we are steering the ship of our life.
>
> Otherwise we feel overloaded, overreact to minor annoyances, and feel like we can never catch up. As far as I'm concerned, one of the best ways is by seeking, and enjoying, solitude . . .
>
> Solitude suggests peacefulness stemming from a state of inner richness. It is a means of enjoying the quiet and whatever it brings, that is satisfying and from which we draw sustenance. It is something we cultivate. Solitude is refreshing; an opportunity to renew ourselves. In other words, it replenishes us.[7]

---

6. Buchholz, Ester, "The call of solitude: How spending time alone can enhance intimacy. Being alone can fuel life," para 2, 3.

7. Marano, Hara Estroff, "Solitude Versus Loneliness," para 1, 2, 8.

To better prepare ourselves for eternity with God, we must first learn to discipline our life. When we learn to be quiet, an act of discipline, we learn to listen. We so often use prayer as a one-sided relationship. God is desirous to speak and teach us. We only need to be willing.

CONSIDER

When the Buddha was asked, "Sir, what do you and your monks practice?" He replied, "We sit, we walk, and we eat." The questioner continued, "But sir, everyone sits, walks, and eats." And the Buddha told him, "When we sit, we *know* we are sitting. When we walk, we *know* we are walking. When we eat, we *know* we are eating."

Buddhists practice a technique that is known as mindfulness. Very simply, mindfulness involves becoming aware of thoughts and actions of the present moment. Although meditative in nature, it is not restrained to classic meditation; rather it is the act of observing reality through a continual mode of awareness. Mindfulness plays a key role in the practice of Buddhism. Right Mindfulness is the seventh element of the Noble Eightfold Path which the Buddhist's believe leads to insight and wisdom. One of the first steps in Buddhist mindfulness is to be aware.

Hundreds of years prior to the creation and development of Buddhism, the Psalmist sings out, "Be still and know (be aware) that I am God" (Psalms 46:10, parenthesis added). Being aware of our reality is nothing new. God has been mindful of reminding us for centuries. We are to be in a continual awareness of God's presence at all times: When we struggle, we know God is with us. When we are blessed, we know it is God who has prospered us. When we pray, we know it is God who responds and speaks to us.

When we consider God, we become aware of him. Consider these verses (emphasis added):

- "But be sure to fear the LORD and serve him faithfully with all your heart; *consider* what great things he has done for you." (1 Samuel 12:24)
- "Listen to this, Job; stop and *consider* God's wonders." (Job 37:14)
- "When I *consider* your heavens, the work of your fingers, the moon and the stars, which you have set in place, what is man that you are mindful of him, the son of man that you care for him?" (Psalms 8:3–9)
- "I will meditate on all your works and *consider* all your mighty deeds." (Psalms 77:12)
- "Whoever is wise, let him heed these things and *consider* the great love of the Lord." (Psalms 107:43)
- "Then I would not be put to shame when I *consider* all your commands." (Psalm 119:6)
- "I meditate on your precepts and *consider* your ways." (Psalms 119:15)
- ". . . and because I *consider* all your precepts right, I hate every wrong path." (Psalm 119:128)
- "*Consider* what God has done." (Ecclesiastes 7:13)

These few verses direct us to be perpetually mindful of God's presence. The persistent problem that plagues most Christians is the distractions of noise, sights, tastes, and other fleshly desires. Writers on the art of meditation state that while preparing to meditate, one should be aware of distractions such as a dog barking, a car passing by, a fan blowing, a refrigerator running, and other noises that seem distracting. The key to blocking out these noises is to recognize that they *are* distractions. Once you have recognized that there is something keeping you from God's presence, acknowledge it and bring your thoughts back to God (Philippians 4:8).

A pivotal question I asked myself was: *Why did God create us?* Are we simply slaves to be held in a perpetual state of longing to be free, and seeking our Master to relieve us of daily burdens? I discovered that God longs for us to know him. How do we know him? Only by spending time with him. This is worship. As we quiet our hearts we can become keenly aware of God's voice and his love for us. God has a passion for us to have a passion for him.

SUNDAY MORNING HIGHS—
MONDAY MORNIN' BLUES

One of my favorite Bible stories is that of Elijah waiting for God on Mt. Horeb (1 Kings 19:11–13). We find throughout the book of Kings that God often speaks to Elijah in a clear concise voice. In 1 Kings 18 and 19, we find God speaking to Elijah, first telling him to go to Mt. Carmel then to Mt. Horeb.

Mt. Carmel was a magnificent event for Elijah. Here, on the top of Mt. Carmel, he would have one of the largest audiences ever in his life. Poised with confidence, he challenges the Baal prophets to a duel. With righteous arrogance, the Baal prophets accept the duel: the first god to rain down fire upon the sacrificial altar was the winner.

The Baal prophets go first and spend all morning and most of the afternoon calling upon their gods. Elijah was thoroughly enjoying this show. At one point he began to taunt them, ". . . shout louder . . . perhaps he is deep in thought or traveling . . . maybe your god is sleeping," (1 Kings 18:27).

After hours of pleading to their gods, they finally give up. Elijah steps forward and calls upon God to act. God does so by performing a mighty miracle. He sends fire down from heaven to consume a waterlogged sacrifice. Immediately the Israelites bow down and worship Jehovah. What a mountain top experience for Elijah.

Elijah, in all of his glory after this event had over 400 Baal prophets killed. We don't know the full emotional state of Elijah during this time, but let's consider this possibility. Previous actions by Elijah show him as a prophet obediently listening to God's voice and doing exactly what God says, with positive results. Each time Elijah moved on to the next adventure confident that God would act and he would reap the rewards of being an obedient prophet. The difference this time is that maybe, just maybe, the events did not end on a happy note as Elijah might have been expecting. He finds himself on the run because Queen Jezebel puts a contract out on him, and her army is in hot pursuit to kill him for the murder of the Baal prophets, and for embarrassing her.

In 1 Kings 19:3, we find that Elijah ". . . was afraid and ran for his life." Elijah, the great prophet, afraid? This seems out of character for Elijah. Where is his trust in God? Could it be that he was living off his mountain top experience and expected God to act a certain way, but he didn't? What happens next is even more intriguing.

Next we see Elijah leaving his servant and running deep into the desert. Jezebel wants him dead and he finds himself a wanted man running for his life. Exhausted, he falls down beneath a tree and cries out to God to let him die. Was Elijah experiencing a great depression? He ran into the desert knowing there would be no water or food there. He is tired, and beaten down. His desire is to die. Does this sound like the Elijah we just read about in previous chapters? Evidently, life isn't turning out the way he thought it would. But God wasn't finished with him. He sends an angel who brings him food and water. Then God instructs him to go to Mt. Horeb.[8]

Mt. Horeb was a forty-day journey from where he was. What was going through his mind during this long trek? Was he looking over his shoulder wondering if Jezebel's men were after him? Was he thinking that this was the last chance for God to prove himself? What we do know is that God didn't give up on him.

After traveling for almost a month and a half, Elijah finally reaches Mt. Horeb. God tells him to go even further, to the top of the mountain and wait there. Now after climbing to the top of this mountain, a very physically demanding trek, he waits. He is mentally, physically, and possibly spiritually exhausted, but he does as he is told, and waits.

We don't know how long he waited before a great wind came and shook the mountain. We do know that

8. Also known as Mt. Sinai, and the Mountain of God.

God was not in the wind. Again Elijah waited. Then a terrible earthquake rocked the mountain like never before, probably knocking him to the ground. God was not in the earthquake. Elijah gets up and once again waits for God. A terrible fire sweeps across the mountain, probably leaving him reeking of smoke. God was not in the fire. I would think by this time, after surviving a tornado, an earthquake, and a forest fire, Elijah may doubt his sanity for being on top of this mountain.

Looking across the vast mountain, now desolate because of fire, Elijah stands up and with all of the strength he has and he waits. Finally, he hears God's voice. Without warning, God passes by whispering in a still, small voice. His waiting brought him an indescribable experience with God.

It is interesting that God gets his attention by whispering. God didn't yell from heaven, He simply grabbed Elijah's attention by quietly speaking to him in a still, small voice. These three simple words in Hebrew have profound significance:

1. Still (damam—daw-man) has the connotation of a whisper or a calm sea as found in Psalms 107:29, "He stilled the storm to a whisper; the waves of the sea were hushed."

2. Small (daq—dak) means fine or thin.

3. Voice (Qwol—kole) is from an unusual root word that means to call aloud as found in Exodus 19:19, ". . . Moses spoke and God answered him with thunder [in his voice]."

God spoke to Elijah in voice loud enough for him to hear (Qwol) but soft enough (daman) that it was calming to his soul, yet he was forced to strain (dak) to listen carefully to God's voice. The word "daq" in this verse has interesting connotations. If something is fine or thin like a strand of hair, you need to concentrate and focus on it. God speaks to Elijah in a way that releases his fears, anxieties, and any unbelief, yet with an unmistakable voice. He let Elijah know without a doubt that it is he who is calling out. His voice is calming, and unique. Elijah hears something, yet he needed to focus and disregard any other distractions to listen to God's unique voice.

How does this story apply to you? Are you going to church Sunday-to-Sunday (your mountaintop), but acting differently throughout the week? Has your life somehow changed in a way you were not expecting? Things didn't turn out as Elijah had expected. He was used to walking away a hero, but he became a fugitive. Sometimes we expect life to treat us the same everyday. When problems arise, are you quick to run away and find the answer on your own (a Humanistic-Christian characteristic) or do you wait on God? Remember that Elijah spent a quiet pilgrimage to Mt. Horeb contemplating his life.

6

Disturbances

THE IDEAL situation for tracking an animal is having ideal weather with ideal conditions. However, for Tom Brown Jr. (*The Tracker*), this was rarely the case. Most of the time the track was a few days old, or rain or snow had disturbed the track. However, it was not impossible to follow the trail even if it has been disturbed.

Tom would carefully examine the track and look for anything that would reveal the true nature of the animal or where the animal was going. He inspected every inch of the track, looking at the how the wind settled the dirt or how deep the track was at the particular time he discovered it. After carefully scrutinizing every aspect of the track he made his conclusions. He didn't hurry, a Humanistic-Christian characteristic, wondering how much time he would lose if he stopped. He knew he would be better equipped to know which way to go if he took the time to stop and examine the disturbance.

Tom's actions were to stop and observe. Our actions should be to stop and allow God to work. As we pray about the disturbance in our life, we need to examine what God can teach us from it. But how many times do we tend to hurry to fix a disturbance in our life instead of waiting to see what it reveals to us?

Many of us are to busy with Humanistic-Christian beliefs to understand that God is calling us to stop and listen. We believe we can do a better job of caring for our lives than God can. I was once given counsel by a dear, elderly Christian lady who suggested that I put feet to my prayers. She truly believed that we needed to help God solve our problems. She didn't understand the command by God (Psalms 46:10) to wait in prayer and have faith that he will, in his way, take care of our disturbances. Waiting and being quiet before God is an act of faith. What a tremendous opportunity God gives us to get to know him better.

THE RESET BUTTON

My younger brother John is a mechanical genius. He can fix almost anything. He amazes me with his insight into mechanics and construction. For nearly thirty years he has worked for a milk-processing plant. While working in the maintenance department, he was called out of bed in the middle of the night to fix a machine that had stopped working. John knew every machine in the plant and was well acquainted with the way they worked. The operators and supervisors explained to John that the machine jammed but they were unable to restart it after un-jamming it. Prior to calling John they spent two hours trying to figure out the problem with no avail.

John walked around the machine, examined it closely, then stood back with the supervisors and other workers and studied the machine. After pondering the situation, John turned to the operator and asked if he had pushed the restart button. Much to his embarrassment, he shyly answered, "No." He pushed the button and the machine came to life. John knew the problem because he took time to examine the situation, and he spent time getting to know the machines.

As Christians, we need to take time to examine our situations and to know God. Sometimes we make disturbances in our life more complicated than they really are. When in reality all we need to do is seek, wait, and sometimes just push the reset button.

"DOING" GOD'S WORK

We sometimes run as far as we can to avoid waiting. Often, where we run is straight to church. Thomas Merton addresses this with raw candor:

> There are men dedicated to God whose lives are full of restlessness and who have no real desire to be alone. They admit that exterior solitude is good in theory . . . In practice their lives are devoured by activities and strangled with attachments. Interior solitude is impossible for them. They fear it . . . They are great promoters of useless work. They love to organize meetings, and banquets, and conferences, and lectures. They print circulars, write letters, talk for hours on the telephone in order that they may gather a hundred people together in a large room where they . . . roar at one another and clap their hands and stagger home at last patting one another on the back with assurance they have all done great things to spread the Kingdom of God.[1]

1. Merton, *New Seeds of Contemplation*, 83.

There can be no contemplation, no contentment, and no consideration of God's grace and love for us when we are so busy *doing*. Entering into the spiritual realm is difficult, if not impossible, without pause. How then can we enter into God's presence when we have a restless spirit that causes us to be devoured *by activities and strangled with attachments*?

DUO-TASKING

In our crazy, busy, A.D.D. culture we brag about multitasking. Even the origination of the name, multiple tasking, is compounded to make it easier to pronounce. Doing multiple tasks at one time can seriously affect your ultimate goal because each time you introduce a new object of attention into what you are doing, you dilute your attention on any one object.[2] If our goal is to have an intimate relationship with God, how do we accomplish this when we dilute our attention with the soft glow of our computer screen, while changing the channel on our TV, while talking to our friends on our cell phones?

Our culture has created a multitasking environment. Sometimes we need to multitask, and sometimes we need to stop. Multitasking can be addicting. Longing for God often takes a back seat to a busy lifestyle and we become God-Defecit. We become passionless towards God.

As Christians we should be duo-tasking: doing two things at the same time. We live in a physical world, but as Christians we have access to the spiritual world. Duo-

2. Hallowell, Crazybusy: *Overstretched, Overbooked, and about to snap!*, 20.

tasking is the obligation of every believer to live in the physical world and to be constantly aware of God. Many of us try to duo-task only when we are in a fellowship gathering. Throughout the week we forget that God is always waiting for us to be used by him. People are hurting and needful all around us, sometimes within arm's reach. How can we be listening for God's purpose if we are only living in the physical world? Whether at work, recreation, or alone, we should be tuned in to God.

Jesus is the model we use to live a lifestyle of worship. Everything about Jesus was duo-tasking. He lived in the physical world but was continually listening to his Father. The story of the Samaritan woman he meets at a well (John 4) is a prime example of duo-tasking. He meets her (physical world) and while they are talking Jesus is listening to his Father (spiritual world). God reveals to Jesus that this woman has been married five times and the man she is living with is not her husband. If Jesus is able to Duo-task, why shouldn't we? Be available. Listen.

DESSERT

Many of us today want to live on dessert. We love to experience an energy filled *worship* service every Sunday, but seem to overlook the more disciplined aspects God calls us to. One reason we attend church services is because God says, ". . . let us consider how we may spur one another on toward love and good deeds, not giving up meeting together, as some are in the habit of doing, but encouraging one another . . ." (Hebrews 10:24–25). But is this the real reason we meet together?

Francois Fenelon was the court preacher for King Louis XIV of France in the 17th century. One Sunday when the king and his attendants arrived at the chapel for the regular service no one else was there but the preacher. King Louis demanded, "What does this mean?" Fenelon replied, "I had published that you would not come to church today, in order that Your Majesty might see who serves God in truth and who flatters the King." Do we meet to create an image of ourselves for others to behold, or do we truly meet to encourage and be encouraged?

GOD STEALING TIME (GST)

Time is either an obstacle we abuse by missing out on God's amazing blessings, or it is the wonderful gift we accept to sit in quiet with him. Everyday we are offered a choice to use our time wisely. What we choose is a reflection of our spiritual temperament. Do you steal valuable time from God? Do you choose to be with God or do you choose to be without God?

The paradox is that we hesitate to become absorbed by God in fear of losing out on momentary afflictions of pleasure. We would rather miss time with him than our favorite TV show. When we steal time from God we become desensitized to the passion God has for us.

THE ATHLETE

In the following verses Paul refers to the rigors of athletes to illustrate the point on how to continually keep our passion alive for God:

- "Do you not know that in a race all the runners run, but only one gets the prize? Run in such a way as to get the prize. Everyone who competes in the games goes into strict training. They do it to get a crown that will not last; but we do it to get a crown that will last forever. Therefore I do not run like a man running aimlessly; I do not fight like a man beating the air. No, I beat my body and make it my slave so that after I have preached to others, I myself will not be disqualified for the prize." (1 Corinthians 9:24–27)

- "Therefore, since we are surrounded by such a great cloud of witnesses, let us throw off everything that hinders and the sin that so easily entangles, and let us run with perseverance the race marked out for us." (Hebrews 12:1)

- "Similarly, anyone who competes as an athlete does not receive the victor's crown except by competing according to the rules." (2 Timothy 2:5)

- "I have fought the good fight, I have finished the race, I have kept the faith." (2 Timothy 4:7)

The comparison Paul is referring to is that of an Olympic athlete. The athletes of this time period aren't much different than those of our contemporary athletes. Fame and fortune follow the champion. The Roman and Greek athlete trained rigorously to obtain a victory so coveted it could mean early retirement, wealth, and fame for the rest of their lives.

Generally, Olympic events were three days long. In some cities, the winner of the Olympic games was treated with such prestige that a hole would be made in the outer wall of the city and the victor would be led in on a chariot with four white horses. Depending on who the ruler was, some champions had statues erected, at the cost of the government, and strategically placed in the busiest part of the city.

The only name ever recorded at an Olympic event was the winner. There was no second or third place, no bronze or silver. Therefore, the goal of the athlete was to commit to a regimented, disciplined life of training to win. Each day was filled with a planned, organized schedule of events. His meals were planned, his exercise demanding, and most importantly, he must abstain from anything that might corrupt his goal. He pushed his body to the limits of endurance. He kept his goal focused on the prize. A person with a strong commitment to thorough and extensive training could obtain riches by adhering to a regimented lifestyle.

The correlation Paul draws is that of a spiritual versus a physical training:

- The Olympic victor was given a crown made of olive leaves. A crown that eventually would wilt and die not like a crown of gold.

- A runner must run an Olympic event with his eyes focused on the course track for any ruts, stones or any other objects that might hinder his performance. He must also know where his opponents are at all times. If he were to look into the crowd he may lose his balance or run off the track. Likewise, we are to focus on God and listen to Him. When we try to 'do' things for God we take our eyes off the track.

- Boxing was an event at some Olympiads. If a boxer was not in shape or thoroughly trained in the art of boxing, he could easily throw punches that connected with nothing but air. Paul's visual is of a boxer swinging his arms and flailing at the air. Picture Jerry Lewis trying to fight Evander Holyfield. The trained boxer is in top physical condition and prepared to go the distance with his opponent. When we abstain from TV for time with God or spend more time in prayer than Tweeting, when we fast or give financially to those in need when we are struggling ourselves, then we are disciplining our 'spiritual' bodies.

We learn a great deal about lifestyle worship with the athlete analogy. We are to focus on the goal of eternal life with God. With that in mind, we need to discipline our spiritual life. More importantly, Paul makes the distinction that we are to covet God and live a lifestyle of worship.

Discipline means change. Sometimes it is difficult for us to open our minds to new ideas, even if we know they are the right things for us. One reason we don't make the right changes in our life is the cost of doing something like praying, which means concentrating on something other than the television or computer. Discipline equals the expenditure of energy.

WORSHIPPERS WHO WORSHIP

How do we reconcile lifestyle worship with worship? In chapter eight of the book of Nehemiah, we discover that the Israelites have just finished rebuilding the walls of

Jerusalem. We find the people gathered together standing in the square, and that they were of one accord or "one man" (just as the believers were in Acts 2). Ezra brought out the Book of the Law and began to read from it. When he finished he blessed God, and in unison, all of the people shouted, "Amen! Amen!"[3] which means: *so be it!* Or *we are in agreement!* With that they fell to the ground and worshipped God (*proskunetes*). With reckless abandonment to their outward appearance, they fell in the dust, the dirt, and the mud. They weren't looking around to see who was watching, they simply worshipped God. They were at church.

HOW-TO

Have you heard people say, "God is the potter and we are the clay?" It's time to be the clay. If we truly want God to mold us, we have to be willing to sacrifice and discipline ourselves. It starts with stopping and ends with listening.

Find time to be alone and listen. The more time you spend alone, the more you will crave it. It may be difficult at first, but it does get easier. Begin by spending a few minutes in the evening or early morning by yourself. If you find it difficult to pray and listen, tell God. Let him know it is hard, but also ask him for the desire to be with him. It will come. Be consistent in your alone time.

---

3. The primitive root word of 'Amen' is *Aman* which has the meaning of: *to be established, to stand firm, to be certain, to believe.* When the Israelites said 'Amen' it was more than *so be it*, they were saying "We believe! We have no doubt!"

Consider the simple blessing on your life: your health, job, family, a car to drive, a home to live in, and clothes to wear. Throughout the day, pause and listen (i.e. at lunch, or breaks, or between meetings). This may sound trivial, but it's a start. God loves it when we acknowledge his blessing and love over us.

Be open to his prompting to speak to someone (duo-tasking) or just be open to listening period. At first this may seem hard, you may have a difficult time discerning his voice. You may not hear anything. Be patient. Remember that an occasional jogger is not ready for a marathon.

Be aware of life. When you are alone with God don't let your surroundings sidetrack you. If you hear a dog bark, or a car pass by, acknowledge the dog bark and the sound of the car. Simply say, "I acknowledge a dog is barking, I hear the sound of the car." By doing this it won't plague you and distract you. Be aware that when unexpected problems arise God is with you and that you have two choices: either you can scurry around like Martha and try to fix the problem yourself (Humanistic-Christian) or you can STOP and be alone with God and seek him (Faith).

LIFESTYLE WORSHIP

It is not wrong for the worship team to practice and lead the church of communal believers in a time of singing to our Father. Nor is it wrong for a pastor to teach a community of believers how to know God better. When we gather as believers in one geographic location at a specified time we should come with expectant hearts. This may be a difficult concept for some. It may mean a change of attitude. Going to church is not about making an appearance or attending just because this particular church has a great worship team. If we all would come expecting the *up there to come down here* and our *spirit touching God's spirit* we would change the history of Christianity. The heart of Christianity is rising to a renewed responsibility to lifestyle worship. Be still. *Know* he is God.

Appendix

God's Voice

Thoughts:

I AM amazed at the clarity of the Scripture regarding God's voice. It is so clear that He desires to have a relationship with us, yet we seem to rationalize his voice through pastors, evangelists, friends, and other means of communication. This is not to say that he is unable to speak to us through others, but if we would stop and look at what history has to say about God speakin

G TO us, it is obvious that he is trying to get our attention. The following verses are not a complete and exhaustive list pertaining to God's voice, but a few of my favorite verses. I hope you enjoy them too. The word voice is italicized to add emphasis.

OLD TESTAMENT

EXODUS 15:26

". . . if you listen carefully to the *voice* of the LORD your God and do what is right in his eyes, if you pay attention to his commands and keep all his decrees, I will not bring on you any of the diseases I brought on the Egyptians, for I am the LORD, who heals you."

Exodus 19:19

". . . and the sound of the trumpet grew louder and louder. Then Moses spoke and the *voice* of God answered him."

Deuteronomy 5:22

"These are the commandments the LORD proclaimed in a loud *voice* to your whole assembly there on the mountain from out of the fire, the cloud and the deep darkness; and he added nothing more. Then he wrote them on two stone tablets and gave them to me."

Deuteronomy 30:20

" . . . and that you may love the LORD your God, listen to his *voice*, and hold fast to him. For the LORD is your life, and he will give you many years in the land he swore to give to your fathers, Abraham, Isaac and Jacob."

1 Samuel 15:22

"But Samuel replied: 'Does the LORD delight in burnt offerings and sacrifices as much as in obeying the *voice* of the LORD? To obey is better than sacrifice, and to heed is better than the fat of rams.'"

2 Samuel 22:14

"The LORD thundered from heaven; the *voice* of the Most High resounded."

1 Kings 19:12

" . . . and after the earthquake a fire; but the LORD was not in the fire: and after the fire a still small *voice*."

1 Kings 19:13

"When Elijah heard it, he pulled his cloak over his face, went out, and stood at the mouth of the cave. Then a *voice* said to him, 'What are you doing here, Elijah?'"

Job 37:2

"Listen! Listen to the roar of his *voice*, to the rumbling that comes from his mouth."

Job 37:4

"After that comes the sound of his roar; he thunders with his majestic *voice*. When his *voice* resounds, he holds nothing back."

Job 37:5

"God's *voice* thunders in marvelous ways; he does great things beyond our understanding."

Psalm 29:3

"The *voice* of the LORD is over the waters; the God of glory thunders, the LORD thunders over the mighty waters."

Psalm 29:4

"The *voice* of the LORD is powerful; the *voice* of the LORD is majestic."

Psalm 29:5

"The *voice* of the LORD breaks the cedars; the LORD breaks in pieces the cedars of Lebanon."

Psalm 29:7

"The *voice* of the LORD strikes with flashes of lightning."

Psalm 29:8

"The *voice* of the LORD shakes the desert; the LORD shakes the Desert of Kadesh."

Psalm 95:7, 8

" . . . for he is our God and we are the people of his pasture, the flock under his care. Today, if you hear his *voice*, do not harden your hearts . . ."

Isaiah 6:8

"Then I heard the *voice* of the Lord saying, 'Whom shall I send? And who will go for us?' And I said, "Here am I. Send me!"

Isaiah 30:21

"Whether you turn to the right or to the left, your ears will hear a *voice* behind you, saying, 'This is the way; walk in it.'"

Isaiah 33:3

"At the thunder of your *voice*, the peoples flee; when you rise up, the nations scatter."

Ezekiel 43:2

" . . . and I saw the glory of the God of Israel coming from the east. His *voice* was like the roar of rushing waters, and the land was radiant with his glory."

Haggai 1:12

"Then Zerubbabel son of Shealtiel, Joshua son of Jehozadak, the high priest, and the whole remnant of the people obeyed the *voice* of the LORD their God and the message of the prophet Haggai, because the LORD their God had sent him. And the people feared the LORD."

NEW TESTAMENT

MATTHEW 17:5

"While he was still speaking, a bright cloud enveloped them, and a *voice* from the cloud said, 'This is my Son, whom I love; with him I am well pleased. Listen to him!'"

MARK 1:11

"And a *voice* came from heaven: 'You are my Son, whom I love; with you I am well pleased.'"

JOHN 3:29

"The bride belongs to the bridegroom. The friend who attends the bridegroom waits and listens for him, and is full of joy when he hears the bridegroom's *voice*. That joy is mine, and it is now complete."

JOHN 5:25

"I tell you the truth, a time is coming and has now come when the dead will hear the *voice* of the Son of God and those who hear will live."

JOHN 10:3

"The watchman opens the gate for him, and the sheep listen to his *voice*.He calls his own sheep by name and leads them out."

John 10:4

"When he has brought out all his own, he goes on ahead of them, and his sheep follow him because they know his *voice*."

John 10:5

"But they will never follow a stranger; in fact, they will run away from him because they do not recognize a stranger's *voice*."

John 10:27

"My sheep listen to my *voice*; I know them, and they follow me."

John 12:30

"Jesus said, "This *voice* was for your benefit, not mine."

Acts 7:31

"When he saw this, he was amazed at the sight. As he went over to look more closely, he heard the Lord's *voice*."

Acts 9:4

"He fell to the ground and heard a *voice* say to him . . ."

Hebrews 3:15

"As has just been said: 'Today, if you hear his *voice*, do not harden your hearts as you did in the rebellion.'" [Psalm 95:7,8]

2 Peter 1:17

"For he received honor and glory from God the Father when the *voice* came to him from the Majestic Glory, saying, 'This is my Son, whom I love; with him I am well pleased.'"

2 Peter 1:18

"We ourselves heard this *voice* that came from heaven when we were with him on the sacred mountain."

Revelation 1:10

"On the Lord's Day I was in the Spirit, and I heard behind me a loud *voice* like a trumpet . . ."

Revelation 1:15

"His feet were like bronze glowing in a furnace, and his *voice* was like the sound of rushing waters."

Revelation 3:20

"Here I am! I stand at the door and knock. If anyone hears my *voice* and opens the door, I will come in and eat with him, and he with me."

Glossary

1. **Alternative Worship**—Usually refers to an approach to Christian worship and worship planning that emphasizes decentralized leadership, congregational participation, multi-sensory experience, ritual, and narrative form. (Source: http://en.wikipedia.org/wiki/Alternative_worship)

2. **Baby Boomers**—The name for a demographic group born in the United States, from 1943 through 1960 during the economic prosperity following World War II. (From the following sources: Encyclopedia Britannica, http://www.answers.com/, and http://www.cesse.org)

3. **Church Growth Consultants**—Consultants who are paid to ". . . to enhance the efforts of local churches, regional judicatories, and denominations in the task of disciple making [and] . . . to provide practical resources to help pastors, churches, and individuals reach their potential for Christ; to promote spiritual growth in churches, thereby leading Christians to maturity and lost people to Christ; and to equip pastors so they can equip their church members to do the work of the ministry."(Source: Definition is a collaboration of various websites including: http://www.churchgrowth.net/aboutus/mission_statement.htm;

http://www.churchgrowth.org/mission.html; http://www.wls.wels.net/library/Essays/ Authors/)

4. **Communal Worship**—A setting for a community of Believers to partake in a unified experience of worshipping God. (Source: Author)

5. **Contemplation**—The concentration on spiritual things as a form of private devotion; a state of mystical awareness of God's being; an act of considering with attention; to separate something from its environment; (Source: Merriam-Webster Online Dictionary and http://en.wikipedia.org/wiki/Contemplation)

6. **Cultural Worshipologists**—Experts, who respond to the controversial problems associated with postmodern worship, usually restricted to the connectivity of Church Services. Music, environment, and personnel are the most common problems Cultural Worshipologists address. (Source: Author)

7. **Duo-Tasking**—The ability of all Believers to continually be aware of both the physical world and spiritual world at the same time. (Source: Author)

8. **Emerging Church**—The emerging church (also known as the emergent church movement) is a Christian movement of the late 20th and early 21st century whose participants seek to live their faith in modern society by emulating Jesus Christ irrespective of Christian religious traditions. (Source: http://en.wikipedia.org/wiki/Emergingchurch)

9. **Fluid Worship**—The utilization of unorthodox methods and mediums for worship during communal gatherings. (Source: Author).

10. **Generation X**—A term used in demographics, the social sciences, and more broadly in popular culture. It generally consists of persons born between 1960 and 1980. (Source—Various websites: http://en.wikipedia.org/wiki/Generation_X, http://users.metro2000.net/~stabbott/genxintro.htm, http://www.jour.unr.edu/outpost/specials/genx.overvw1.html http://www.cesse.org)

11. **Humanistic-Christian**—A Christian's attitude to seek, solve, pursue, and maintain life within individual parameters and power, void of faith. (Source: Author)

12. **Method of Creation (M.O.C.)**—A methodical and systematic process used to create a worship experience, usually prepared for Sunday gatherings usually utilizing a musical and/or a theatrical medium. (Source: Author)

13. **Mysticism**—The conviction that Believers can have an intimate relationship with God. (Source: Author)

14. **Nexters**—Also known as Gen Nexters and occasionally referred to as Generation Y. The name for a demographic group born in the United States, from 1980 to 2000. (Source: http://www.cesse.org)

15. **Open Church**—The belief that (1) The Church needs to get back to the basics of the New Testament Church, (2) That Christians must take a more ac-

tive role in their local fellowships, (3) Turn the Communal Gatherings into "Participatory" gatherings rather then "Spectator" events, (4) Create an environment that actually allows people to use their gifts (5) To close the gap of a Pastor-centered fellowship to an equitable Pastor- Parishioner Fellowship. (Source: http://www.openchurch.com/)

16 **Sophist**—A class of ancient Greek teachers of rhetoric, philosophy, and the art of successful living famous for their adroit subtle and allegedly often specious reasoning. Also, a name for a person who uses clever but false arguments. Plato was an outspoken critic of the Sophists due to their materialistic lifestyle. Plato characterized them as "superficial manipulators of rhetoric and dialectic." The word 'Sophist' eventually became a derogatory connotation. (Sources: Merriam Webster Dictionary, Compact Oxford English Dictionary, and The American Heritage Dictionary)

Bibliography

Barna Research Group. "Americans Describe Sources of Spiritual Fulfillment and Frustration." No pages. Online: http://www.barna.org/barna-update/article/5-barna-update/199-americans-describe-sources-of-spiritual-fulfillment-and-frustration

Becker, Margaret. *Coming Up For Air*. Colorado Springs: Navpress Publishing Group, 2006.

Best, Harold. "Worship, Faith, Grace, and Music Making Event: Worship! LA (Christian Worship Conference." No pages. Online: http://worshipinfo.com/quicktakes/best3.htm

Boschman, LaMar. *A Passion For His Presence*. Shippensberg. PA: Revival Press, 2003

Bradshaw, David and James H. Rutz, "The Big Picture: A Surprise-laden Survey of the 30 Foremost Movements of God in America." No pages. Online: http://www.myideafactory.net/bigpict.html

Brown, Tom Jr. *The Tracker*. NY: Berkley Publishing Group, 1978

Bucholz, Ester, "The call of solitude: How spending time alone can enhance intimacy. Being alone can fuel life." No pages. Online: http://www.psychologytoday.com/articles/199802/the-call-solitude.

Cimino, Richard, and Don Lattin. *Shopping For Faith: American Religion in the New Millennium*. San Francisco: Jossey-Bass Inc., Publishers, 1998

Dekker, Ted. *The Slumber of Christianity: Awakening A Passion for Heaven on Earth*. Nashville, TN: Thomas Nelson, Inc., 2005

Drucker, Peter. *Post-Capitalist Society*. NY: HarperBusiness, 1993

Foster, Richard. *Celebration of Discipline: The Path to Spiritual Growth*. NY: HarperCollins, 1978

———. *Prayer: finding the heart's true home*. San Francisco: Harper, 1992

———. *Devotional Classics: selected readings for individuals and groups*. NY: HarperCollins, 1993

Giglio, Louie. *The Air I Breathe*. Sisters, OR: Multnomah Publishers, Inc., 2003

Guiness, Os, "Sounding Out the Idols of Church Growth." No pages. Online: http://gospel-culture.org.uk/guinness.htm

Hallowell, Edward. *Crazybusy: Overstretched, Overbooked, and about to snap! Strategies for coping in a world gone ADD*. NY: Ballantine Books, 2006

Hanh, Thich Nhat. *Living Buddha, Living Christ*. NY: Riverhead Books, 1995

Hill, Andrew E. *Enter His Courts With Praise!* Grand Rapids: Baker Books, 2002

Kundtz, David. *Stopping: how to be still when you have to keep going*. Berkeley, CA: Conari Press, 1998

Kushner, Harold S. *Who Needs God*. NY: Pocket Books, 1989

Lawrence, Brother. *The Practice of The Presence of God / Brother Lawrence; and, The Way of Perfection/ Teresa of Avila*. Nashville: Thomas Nelson, Inc., 1999

Lexington-Herald, "A Revival Account Asbury 1970," May 2008.

Lowrie, Walter. *Kierkegaard's Attack Upon Christendom: 1854–1855*. Princeton, NJ: University Press, 1968

Marano, Hara Estroff. "Solitude Versus Loneliness." *Psychology Today* (July 2003). No pages. Online: http://www.psychologytoday.com/articles/200308/what-is-solitude

Merton, Thomas. *New Seeds of Contemplation*. NY: New Directions Books, 1961

Ortberg, John. *God Is Closer Than You Think: This Can Be the Greatest Moment of Your Life Because This Moment Is the Place Where You Can Meet God*. Grand Rapids: Zondervan, 2005

Peterson, David. *Engaging With God, A Biblical Theology of Worship*. Grand Rapids: William B. Eerdmans, 1992

Pinckney, Coty. "The Essence of Worship." No pages. Online: http://blog.worship.com/worship/2006/08/the_essence_of_.html

Redman, Matt. (2001). *The Unquenchable Worshipper*. Ventura, CA: Regal Books.

Rogers, Dan. (n.d.). *In Search of an Acceptable Christian Corporate Worship*. Online: http://www.wcg.org/lit/spiritual/worship/worship2.htm

Rogers, Jay. "A Revival Account Asbury 1970" (March 2008). No pages. Online: http://www.forerunner.com/forerunner/X0585_Asbury_Revival_1970.html

Webber, Robert. "Worship (Part 1)." No pages. Online: http://bible.org/seriespage/worship-part-1-john-41-26

Willard, Dallas. *The Spirit of Disciplines: understanding how God changes lives.* San Francisco: Harper, 1991

Zuck, John. "What is Christian Mysticism?" No pages. Online: http://www.frimmin.com/faith/mysticismintro.html

www.ingramcontent.com/pod-product-compliance
Lightning Source LLC
Chambersburg PA
CBHW071437160426
43195CB00013B/1935